A Change Is Gonna Come

A Change Is Gonna Come

Reinvention in the City of Second Chances

Essays, Stories, and Poems

Volume 10—Las Vegas Writes

Edited by Scott Dickensheets
and Geoff Schumacher

HUNTINGTON PRESS
LAS VEGAS, NEVADA

A Change Is Gonna Come
Reinvention in the City of Second Chances

Published by
  Huntington Press
  3665 Procyon Street
  Las Vegas, NV 89103
  Phone (702) 252-0655
  e-mail: books@huntingtonpress.com

Edited by: Scott Dickensheets and Geoff Schumacher

Contributing Writers: Jennifer Battisti, Steve Bornfeld, Harry R. Fagel, Dayvid Figler, Lonn M. Friend, A.D. Hopkins, Veronica Klash, Oksana Marafioti, Mike Prevatt, Elizabeth Quiñones-Zaldaña, Vogue Robinson, Erin Ryan, Steve Sebelius, and Amanda Skenandore

ISBN: 978-1-944877-37-8
$13.95us

Cover Design: Christopher Smith
Production & Design: Laurie Cabot

Acknowledgments

The Las Vegas Writes Project 2019 is supported by public and private funding for the literary arts through Nevada Humanities, the National Endowment for the Humanities, the Nevada Center for the Book, Nevada State Library Archives and Public Records, Institute of Museum and Library Services, the Nevada Arts Council, the National Endowment for the Arts, the Las Vegas-Clark County Library District, Test Site Projects, and Huntington Press. The program receives support with readings and conversations hosted at venues that support the literary arts from, the city of Las Vegas Office of Cultural Affairs, The Writer's Block Book Store, and the Las Vegas Book Festival at the Historic 5th Street School, Las Vegas, Nevada.

Contents

Introduction

The Next, Next New Thing

By Scott Dickensheets

In the spring of 2019, artist and photographer Bryan McCormack exhibited a batch of stereoscopic cameras and photos — stereographic: doubled images that, when looked at through the right lenses, appeared in 3D — in the Las Vegas office of Nevada Humanities. He showed a lot of equipment, from 19th century lenses to the View-Masters you remember from childhood, and a lot of images. Relevant to the concerns of this book were a batch taken during John C. Fremont's pioneering explorations of Southern Nevada in the mid-1800s. Let's look at three, all, not coincidentally, depicting Native Americans. One shows a group of native men seated in a loose semicircle. It's titled "The Old Gamblers." In another, a youngish woman is topless. In the third, a man wears buckskins indigenous to a Plains tribe that lives many hundreds of miles away; Fremont had spruced him up this way because he knew the buckskins symbolized "Indians" to the East Coast audience he was very keen on peddling his stereoscopic images to.

Gambling, sexual titillation, imported culture, phony narratives serving commercial interests — Las Vegas was already being reinvented before there was a Las Vegas to reinvent. (Leave it to a colonialist white guy to get *that* ball rolling.)

In the years since, the idea of reinvention has truly become one of the load-bearing beliefs about Las Vegas, this city of second chances. It's the hot core of gambling's appeal, of course: upcycling your life with a turn of the cards, a roll of the dice, the spin of a *Downton Abbey* slot machine. Who might you become with a Megabucks win in your money belt? What is a weekend bender in Sin City if not a chance to try on the sorts of personae that won't fly in Pig's Knuckle, Nebraska?

And from the Strip, this reinvention mojo has seeped into the wider psychology of the valley. It's surely some of what brought a guy named Arthur Jones to Las Vegas back in the 1980s, where he worked as a bookie under a different name for some twenty-five years after disappearing and being declared dead in Chicago. Every now and then you'll see a headline like that — some embezzler from New Jersey is captured while trying to start a new life in Las Vegas. It never fails to not surprise me. I mean, where else would you go? New Orleans, I suppose, if you can stand the humidity and love jambalaya. But very often it's Vegas.

Of course, most reinvention is neither sinister nor worthy of note; it's just everyday personal growth, as we work to extend or escape our narratives and histories. We all do it to one extent or another. I barely recognize the me of my mid-thirties, so many iterations have I gone through since then. You, too, I'm sure. "I have a nudging voice inside telling me there is something else to be, beyond that which I have been, and beyond that, something else," writes Cecila Dintino in a *Psychology Today* blog post. Or, as onetime Las Vegan Gregory Crosby put it in his poem "So Long, Erato": "Who are you now if not someone else?"

And yet, thankfully for the sake of this book, some stories do warrant a telling. Maybe because reinvention was dramatically foisted upon someone, as with the subject of Erin Ryan's essay; or because a guy fell both gratefully and ruefully into his new life, as did Steve Bornfeld; or because a life is shaken by someone else's change, as is the protagonist of Amanda Skenandore's short story; or because someone, while appearing to shape-shift in a wildly fluctuating time, is revealed to have not changed at all, as in Steve Sebelius' report; or, as in Oksana Marafioti's short story, someone …

well, you'll just have to experience that one on your own.

For all of the off-the-wall plotlines, unbelievable characters, tragicomic developments, civic pratfalls, and occasional moments of beauty and epiphany that crowd the picture of Las Vegas, perhaps its true and abiding theme, from the moment Fremont spurred his horse into the valley and right up to the baccarat cards falling as you read this, is *change*. Implacable and relentless, it's most blatantly at work these days in the terraforming of our cityscape, from the Tony Hsieh'd Downtown to the Raiders' stadium. And you'll find some of that in this book, in Jennifer Battisti's poem, for one. But it's our hope that these stories, essays, and poems also reflect that shaping force in the more intimate, human-scaled ways that will resonate in your own life.

As with all books, the one you're holding is the product of more hands than just those of its writers and editors, and we would be remiss not to mention some of them. (And we do hate to be remiss.) As always, the team at Nevada Humanities deserves a Hulk-size fist bump for continuing to support this project, which for ten volumes now has attempted to celebrate the breadth, depth, and quality of literary talent in Las Vegas. Likewise, Anthony Curtis, Deke Castleman, and their Huntington Press crew have been exemplary publishing partners for many of these volumes. Big ups to those who have chipped in in other ways, as detailed on the Acknowledgments page you probably skipped. (Take a moment to go back.) And a hearty thanks to Christopher Smith, art director of *Desert Companion* magazine, for designing the book's cover.

Across ten anthologies — a milestone hardly imaginable at the outset — Las Vegas Writes has showcased dozens of worthy local writers. And it turns out that one of the great joys of the project has been our realization that no matter how many volumes ultimately comprise the series, Las Vegas will never run out of writers to fill them. ◆

The Phoenecian

By Dayvid Figler
(Poem)

I.
Frank Lloyd Wright was down on his luck in 1965.

Recently arrived in Las Vegas
(though having died some years earlier)
nothing seemed to be going Wright.

Commissioned to build
the Phoenix Hotel and Casino
on the cursed site of the original El Rancho Vegas,
things had already fallen apart.

He put his entire
upfront

The Phoenecian

on red, Friday night,
but the roulette ball landed on
    normal, Saturday morning.

He wagered building after building on
    zero;
every single time it came up 28,
Saturday night.

    What were the odds?

Frank Lloyd Wright was busted and disgusted.

He was in deeper than he ever thought.
Suckered by the dreams and schemes
of a contingent of
questionable reputations
from St. Louis, and St. Martin

    (patron saint of hairdressers).

Oh, what a comedy team.

Never was there a chance
    the project would fly.

Frank Lloyd Wright slumped low,
in the oversized booth of the Frontier Hotel's
Pioneer Cafe,
elbows on the table,
Prairie-style.

>A stack of dollar-sized pancakes
>$1.25
>A large prune juice
>$0.90
>One egg (poached)
>$0.70
>One hot cup of Postum
>$0.30

All comped.

He cradled his head in his hands
fingers working into the silvery sheen
of his hair,
face down in the menu.

CREAMED CHIPPED BEEF on White Toast ... $2.65

Over and over, again and again.

The telephone rang
on the shelf
behind his booth.

The telephone rang, again and again.

(Pick up. Pick up. It's Beldon Katleman!)

II.
On November 22, 1989,

Georgia O'Keefe was frail
but thrilled
to see the Mirage open to the public.

(She, too, had died years earlier).

Soon she was sitting
in the middle of a volcano,
waiting for an audience
with a blind man
about a plan
loosely connected
to vending machines.

The excitement around the totality
of these circumstances was palpable.

In her left hand,
held by its remaining fur:
a Big Horn Sheep's head
in a state of advanced decay.

In her right:
a bouquet
of sagebrush with blooms
snatched from the inside
of a dust dervish,
mere blocks from the Strip.

Georgia O'Keefe fondly remembered
an evening with Frank Lloyd Wright in 1942
at the University of Wisconsin.
The lightness of conversation.
Presence.
Coquettishness in subtext, only.
Later, on a train to Chicago, she would
unsuccessfully stutter her thoughts
in written correspondence.

End them by saying, as after and before thought:

"Will you give a very quiet greeting and
thanks to the beautiful wife

Sincerely,
        Georgia O'Keefe"

How she wished it was Frank
who was dropping into the volcano this day.

She breathed, heavily.
Her stomach rumbled.

III.
Backstage,
Slim Whitman is gearing up
for the first night of his residency
At the Kaos
        (pronounced kä,äs)
                nightclub at the Palms.

It is December 31, 2027.

Dayvid Figler

Slim Whitman is praying,
as is his ritual.

This will likely be his last opportunity
to resonate with the young people

(having passed away in 2013 with little fanfare).

His driver's license says he will be 104
before Capricorn turns to Aquarius.

This is Kaos' last gambit.
It opened on April Fool's Day 2019
to great celebration.

       Many tweeks and twerks later,
       it is on fumes.

       Much is riding on this Slim chance.

The only remaining artifact from Kaos' start is
       Damien Hirst's "Demon With A Bowl."

When it arrived, it was derided as derivative
by every art critic in Las Vegas.

"Robot 'David' with a Bigger Unit."
"Treasures from the Blecch of the Unbelievable."
"The Amazing Colossal Man Has His Revenge on Vegas"
"More Venetian Nonsense Thrust Upon Us."
"Headless Man Found in Topless Casino."
"Load that Bowl: I'll Have What He's Having."

The people didn't care.
Soon Hirst became the toast of the town.

A "Key to the County" from
          Commissioner "Tick" Segerblom.
A parade on Mel Tormé Way.
Donny Osmond even wrote and recorded a song called
          "Welcome to Our Fabulous Ashtray."
                    (feat. Dan Reynolds)
The Golden Tiki bar celebrated by installing
          a pre-shrunken Hirst head atop bamboo ephemera.

Gangly masses of local art lovers
          smashed all rival installations.

Jeff Koons' "Popeye,"
          Wynn Hotel.
                    Toppled.

Henry Moore's "Reclining Connected Forms,"
    Aria Hotel.
             Disentangled.
James Turrel's "Akhob,"
        (3rd Floor, Louis Vuitton, Crystals Mall)
             White Washed.
Yayoi Kusama's "Infinity Mirrored Room,"
    Bellagio Hotel.
             Hammered.
Ugo Rondinone's "Seven Magic Mountains,"
    somewhere near Primm.
             Fed to Giant Goldfish.

Slim Whitman does his vocal exercises
    in a green room with a star on the door.

    Yodel Lay Hee Hoo.
    Yodel Lay Hee Hoo.
    Yodel Lay Hee Hoo.

Each "hoo" a step on
    a reverberating scale, three octaves high.

He stares into the mirror.
Personal effects, strewn about within reach:

Mustache wax.
A multitude of kerchiefs.
Gonzo Natural Magic Suit Stain Remover.
A "Lucky Rainbow" mini Troll Doll.
Black & White photos of his beloved,
        Alma Geraldine "Jerry" Crist Whitman.
Five different brands of hairspray.

Slim knows this is a big night.
Three million locals are outside waiting to
        hit the dance floor.
56 Million tourists are outside waiting to
        hit the dance floor.
He reflects upon his long affair with the City.
All the records he sold.
        (More than the Beatles and the Dave Clark Five,
                combined).
His on again/off again enmity with Lovelace Watkins.
That one time he saved the Earth from a
        Martian Attack
by singing "Indian Love Call."

(He quietly sobs about how he couldn't protect
        the Landmark).

All of the sudden,

a chimpanzee in a red vest
and a yellow tutu
bursts into the room,
breaking the budding tension.

Slim considers the mirror, one last time.

"You are a whore, darlin'," he says to himself.

IV.
Vaya Con Dios,
My Darling.

It is New Year's Eve
          Day
               welcoming 1968.

I am standing outside Caesars Palace
with my daddy.

My whole hand is wrapped around his index finger.

I am daddy's little girl,
          but I am in love with Evel Knievel.

The Phoenecian

I ride a tricycle with red, white and blue streamers.

This is the moment I feel grown up for the first time.
This is the moment I feel for Las Vegas.
This is the moment of spectacle and spirit.
This is the moment I realize what home means.

The sun was bright.
The air was filled with the smells of liquor.
 Wild Turkey, I imagine, or V.O.

The motorcycle revving so loud it's bouncing off
 the marble statues.
I want to scream full throttle, but I just squeeze
 my daddy's finger harder.
When Evel is in the air my heart stops.

Time stops.

Now, it's twenty years later.
I'm in a poker room with an older woman
 with red hair named Ceil, who is a shill.
She makes $6.50 an hour and keeps any money she wins.

 (Loses any money she loses.)

We make small talk.
The topic of people who come and go.
The singing of Barry Manilow.

Out of the blue, Ceil says,
        "I once did coke with that daredevil."

I don't want to hear the story.

Everybody in Las Vegas once did something with someone.
Everybody in Las Vegas has a plan,
        once they shed their demons.

I drown her out.
Fashion chip towers.
Make magnificent structures on the felt beach.

A guy at the table is telling another guy at the table
        about history.
"Before the Flamingo was the 'El Rancho.'"
But when he says, "El Rancho,"
he sounds like Keanu Reeves pretending to speak
Spanish.
Making up words.

Now, it is ten years later.
I am working
on reinventing
the "Wheel of Fortune."

The slot machine technology is astonishing.
The data is sinister.

I have a virtual Vanna White at my fingertips.
I've programmed her to send you a message,
        letter by letter.

Will you be able to decode it?

♦ ♦ ♦

Sometimes I drive through the desert,
past the signs for the Air Force base.

When summer starts to creep in.
When I'm bored with this town, again.

I love the solitude to regroup.

I want to build a slot machine that pays off in
    self-esteem,
        that's my dream.
I want to pipe soundtracks from underground
New York movies of the '70s and '80s onto the
casino floors.
I want to open a coffee house that serves
    Raspberry Mochas. A poetry hub for cowboys,
    engineers.

Do you see the wildflowers along the side
of the freeway?

Yellow. So much yellow.
Purple blooms on cactus heads.
Red spindles with fragrant jasmine.

I'm driving past the mountain tops.
I don't know if I'm coming or going,
but I'm driving fast.

I knew an animatronic Samuel Clemens, once.

In retrospect, it was a dumb idea,
    but who knows that in the moment? Who dares call
        any idea "dumb" in Las Vegas?

Robot Sam Clemens sat at the bar
and told a tall tale
about being dispatched to Las Vegas
by the Territorial Enterprise
to cover the installation of the

FARO SUICIDE TABLE OF NOBLE GASSES

at the Atomic Number 10 Bar
on Fremont Street.

Sam's pre-recorded track, on a loop,
started and concluded with the phrase,

This story doesn't end well.

Today, I am a regulator.
I walk, invisibly, through many crowds.

Middle-aged men in black, sleeveless Slayer T-shirts.
Pregnant ladies fresh off the Greyhound Bus.
Professional clowns looking for work.
Podcasters building a home studio between gigs.
The soccer complex.
Bartenders with record deals.
The meet-up group from the library.
Starbucks secret shoppers.
The hockey, adorned.
Frankie Moreno's fan club.
2,000 people tabling at a craft fair.
A busload of Culinary Workers.
Customs from McCarran International Airport.

Here, we all have the chance to put our ears
to the ground
and listen for the sleeping buffalo
calling out to the weary traveler,

COME FEEL MY PAIN

I am driving back from the Valley of Fire.
I am bursting with fireworks.
I am brimming with all the secrets.

The Phoenecian

I look in the rear-view mirror and sigh,

"What a way to make a living."

The radio answers back,

"You think this is bad? My mom thinks I'm a cop in LA."

I don't get pulled over.
I buy an Etch-A-Sketch
at a thrift store in Boulder City.

I am home; I shake off the desert dust. The ash.

I watch the last rays of the day
        retreat from my door step,
revel in the cooler air coming
through the open window,
and close my eyes for tomorrow. ◆

The Promised Land

By Steve Bornfeld
(Nonfiction)

Why, Las Vegas?

Why could you reinvent the world of the wife and son who found new life under your skies, but not the father who would have cherished your spiritual cleansing powers most of all? Why could you not scoop up the entire family and hug us all to your neon-tinged bosom?

Because he had to die. Then we could live anew.

Ah, fate, and its infuriating talent: No kiss on the lips comes without a kick in the ass.

I find it almost biblically bittersweet. In flashes of fevered introspection, my heart frames my pique in Old Testament terms: Dad as Moses — if Moses was part Willy Loman/part Sinatra wannabe — barred from The Promised Land that Las Vegas would have been to him (a kind of Canaan with cocktail waitresses) as his wife and son passed through the "Welcome to Fabulous Las Vegas Nevada" gates.

Twenty-five-hundred miles to the east, through decade after decade, Dad grew weary and wearier, slogging along blighted Queens and Bronx streets, peddling cheap wine to ramshackle liquor stores and bug spray to cut-rate supermarkets to support Mom and me — his New York Israelites, if you will, who depended on that paycheck.

It was the lower-middle-class desert he wandered through from the mid-'50s through the mid-'90s, but he gave us enough manna to get by.

Beyond his wife and son, this man lived for one joy: singing professionally — even if only on weekends for badly needed extra manna. Not from a stage so much as from a dinky raised platform, coaxing wedding and bar mitzvah celebrants to do that silly "Hokey Pokey" or croon his heart out on old American Songbook chestnuts, Broadway favorites, and every Crosby/Sinatra standard the idols of his era ever committed to vinyl.

He'd burst into song for any reason. Or no reason. At home. In the car. On crowded elevators. In front of hundreds of brides, grooms, bar mitzvah boys, bat mitzvah girls, and drunken relatives. It lent fleeting sweetness to the sour pressures of his daily grind. It was the Promised Land he coveted.

That was not to be. Because The Lord sayeth to my Moses:

Along that dark, rainswept New York street you are crossing this night, a car is approaching.
You will not see it.
It is speeding.
It will not stop.
It will bring you to me.
And it will set in motion events that will bring your wife and son to The City of Entertainment. A city perfect for you. A city you may not enter.

Moses got a bum deal. So did Dad.

Looking out over my cozy backyard pool in my modest southwest Las Vegas home, I can see him, if only in my mind's eye.

I see this man, a product of the hardscrabble streets of Newark, New Jersey, tanning himself under the Vegas sun. I see the tensions of his body begin to dissipate — those born of a life raised by a cold, uncaring stepfather; of being yanked out of school at the height of the Depression to help pay bills; of scraping by on Arthur Miller's proverbial "shoeshine and a smile"; of keeping away the internal demons braying just beyond the reach of his psyche — usually by singing them away.

I see him slowly, then ecstatically, lower himself into

the blue pool waters, the hardships of his life floating away. Then, happily, he emerges and goes to change into his snappy black tux to do the only job he has now — the only one he ever wanted — performing passionately, in a Vegas lounge, joy radiating from every pore.

Mom and I sit in the audience, beaming.

I see this world as I wanted it to unfold. But no. I've opened my eyes.

Yes, the Las Vegas home is here, the one he could never have imagined being able to afford, but his son could — aided by the court settlement from his violent death. He is buried beneath a hard mound of New Jersey dirt — has been for 25 years — forever freed, at least, of that goddamn stock of booze and bug spray that wound up funding my dreams instead.

I am no longer the younger man who lost his dad, but a wistful older one, accepting life's unsettling ironies and stark inequities, but haunted by them nonetheless.

I am here. He is not.

Damn you, Las Vegas, for the dream denied. And bless you, Las Vegas, for the dream granted.

Life tumbled toward despondency for me in the fall of 1994, when I lost my job as an entertainment reporter in a New York newsroom. Mere weeks later, as the year closed, that car stopped my father's heart and shattered mine into shards. Life became a simple rotation: Take breaks from mourning to be rejected for employment. Then resume grieving.

I was born and raised in New York. I loved New York. I still love New York.

And New York was now the epicenter of my misery, a taunting daily reminder of professional failure and personal pain. I wanted it in my rearview mirror as fast as my rickety old Toyota could put it there. Though I had tried to look after my grieving mom, living down the street, I knew that the cliché of a "fresh start" was the only way I would truly begin to breathe again.

So I accepted a job offer at a newspaper in a city that would come to teach me to appreciate — retroactively — the wonders of Las Vegas ... Chattanooga, Tennessee.

What seemed all too obvious before I left turned out to be even more obvious after I arrived: A smartass New York Jew was not a snug fit in the buckle of the Bible Belt.

On day one in the newsroom, my first new acquaintance welcomed me with this query: "What church do you go to?" When I hesitantly replied that I planned on attending a house of worship called Beth Shalom, he answered: "Oh, you're going to the Jew church?"

Later that day came this exchange with a random stranger: "Are you a Yankee or a damn Yankee?"

"What's the difference between the two?"

"A Yankee passes through, A damn Yankee STAYS."

Ooooh-kay. And during a stop at a gas station/convenience store, the cashier warned me not to leave without paying for a cup of coffee by cautioning: "You don't wanna jew me now, do ya?"

Oy, ya'all.

I lasted 18 months in Chattanooga, my popularity tanking further when my New York Yankees took the Atlanta Braves — the closet major league team to Chattanooga — in six games in the World Series. Yes, I made a couple of friends — one who would even visit me in Vegas years later — but grew weary of the cultural chasms: abandoning the bar-grill with great burgers because of the uncomfortable stares aimed at me by the regulars, settling for various McDonald's and Burger Kings instead; and living in an apartment complex at the foot of a mountain where resided a revered local celebrity — the widow of Byron De La Beckwith, the murderer of civil rights icon Medgar Evers.

I was a conversation piece there. The way I talked. The way I viewed politics, guns, religion, civil rights, even food. (Grits? Really?) Enough.

I had climbed back into the newspaper business. Time to move on — and out. An ad for an assistant features editor position at the *Las Vegas Sun* was my ticket out of Southern not-so-hospitable hospitality. My old rickety Toyota hit the road again. Churches and grits receded. Desert and neon beckoned.

How can a city with such a distinctive personality offer a blank slate to those with start-over-itis? How can it become a spiritual Etch-a-Sketch — just shake it and make it what you want it to be? How could it not drive me to McDonald's when I wanted the better burger at the bar/grill right where I am?

I know that last one because here I am, the weekend before I start my new gig, relaxing at a bar/grill at the corner of Sunset Road and Green Valley Parkway in Henderson.

No one is staring. Not even when I recite the Four Questions — the traditional queries asked during Passover — over a cellphone to my cousin in Dallas, during a Texas-to-Nevada phone Seder.

An ad-hoc Passover. Not something I would have attempted — in public, at least — in Tennessee. But the only look I get is from a barfly who smiles when he hears me speak in broken Hebrew.

A *smile*. What a *mechaye* (Yiddish: a pleasure, a blessing).

Happy to be here, especially after unhooking myself from the Bible Belt, because Las Vegas welcomes me without condition.

Las Vegas makes no cultural demands because it has no pronounced cultural biases. It is America's ultimate immigrant experience, particularly for those of us immigrating from elsewhere in the United States. It cares not at all about my Bronx accent, my politics, my sports teams, my "Jew church," my lack of NRA bona fides. Its restaurants don't offer me grits.

Las Vegas is a mini-melting pot in the tradition of my home state — just like the small-scale Lady Liberty fronting New York-New York hotel. I am not huddled with anyone. I do not arrive among any masses. But I do yearn to breathe free. Best of all, Las Vegas rivals — and arguably, exceeds — the Big Apple for pure thrills and electricity, but feels less brutal, more merciful, in its unspooling of everyday life. Perhaps that's because so many come here to throw off those parts of themselves that suppress joy, if only for a short while — a vibe that suffuses those of us who come to stay.

A place for this Finnegan to begin again.

Not that it's my first howdy-do with Las Vegas.

Decades earlier, as a child, I was brought here for vacation to visit my uncle, a talent agent who booked acts into Caesars Palace and other properties from the Classic Vegas days. Once a singer himself, he became a behind-the-scenes dynamo. He had a home on St. Louis Avenue with his own swimming pool (kidney-shaped, my mom pointed out! ... What was a kidney?) And a tanned face that could have been the model for the Olympic bronze medal. He even was still a performer — we got copious clips in the mail of his performance as Tevye in *Fiddler on the Roof* at Las Vegas Little Theatre.

Though I lacked his ham factor, we shared the entertainment bug, as I had made my career largely as an entertainment journalist. He is gone now — long before I arrived, in fact — but I have connected to that legacy, proudly. Whether booking performers or reporting on their talents, we are succeeding generations in the Vegas entertainment juggernaut.

Globally renowned but suburban-minded — I once heard this town referred to as "Broadway surrounded by Orange County" — Vegas never overpowered me the way New York can. It enticed me, lured me, invited me to attempt accomplishments that in New York seemed absurd to even dream of.

Always a soldier, never a general, I joined the *Las Vegas Sun* as an assistant features editor — my first job above the rank of staff writer at the newspapers I had written for in New York City, upstate New York, Pennsylvania, and Tennessee.

One month after my arrival, the editor who had hired me departed, elevating his petrified second-in-command — who hadn't yet conquered THAT job — to the top post. On the night before the leadership turnover, I slept approximately seven minutes, convinced I would fail — horribly, humiliatingly, devastatingly — in directing an eight-person staff, juggling the pressures of daily deadlines.

I survived Day One. Then Day Two, Then Day 1,095. Three years in the job. I did what I was sure I couldn't do. Thank you, Las Vegas. I hosted a weekly radio show — me, with the Bronx accent that triggered endless Chattanooga giggles. Thank you, Las Vegas. I wrote a couple of plays that were performed at Las Vegas Little Theatre — the same boards trod by my uncle in his Tevye threads. Thank you, Las Vegas.

My byline has migrated to publications throughout this city. Thank you, Las Vegas — after all these years, I am of you.

And yet, it is one experience — one mesmerizing moment of Zen — that defines how the desert reinvented me. One gorgeously sunny day, at the Valley of Fire, I climbed up a cliff to a significant height, planted myself at the edge, cocked my head toward the sky and closed my eyes.

The silence was stunning. And transformative.

A unique quietude, deep and impenetrable, as if you're communing — with God, nature, the universe, yourself — in a way you never have before. In that moment, I thanked the fates for my fate in Las Vegas.

I was not alone …

Dad was dead. I was the only child. And I had left Mom alone in cold, snowy, implacable New York. With the family dog. And her grief. And yes, supportive friends. Even so, they weren't her family. Guilt gnawed at me, especially because, as I later learned, I had underestimated an estimable woman.

You see, the love was always there.

The gratitude was always there.

But the respect — the kind an adult child pays a parent only after life has knocked you around a bit, deflated that youthful arrogance and held a mirror up to your own fallibility — came much later.

Always had she been an especially attentive, unconditionally loving mom, not to mention the ultimate Jewish mother, right down to that peculiar food fetish familiar to most guests of a Jewish hostess. ("You're full? First you'll rest — then you'll eat again.")

She was generous to a fault (always returning from trips with gifts for others), thoughtful to the extreme (notes and phone calls to friends and family, whom she never allowed to drift out of her everyday orbit, distance be damned), and unfailingly cheerful and talkative (to watch her rescue a flagging dinner party was to be awed by the power of social skills).

She and my dad were as devoted to their only child as parents could possibly be. Given all the divorce and abuse soiling modern family life, the child's cup of blessings runneth over.

And yet, the son never saw the mother — a first-generation American raised long before feminism by Eastern European parents and steeped in "traditional values" — as fully her own person.

Sure, she had opinions and expressed them. But she was such a fiercely loyal wife — married to such a fiercely opinionated man — that she always seemed somehow overshadowed, in stark contrast to the emerging "I Am Woman" generation of women with whom her son had grown up.

Although she learned to drive, she depended heavily on her husband to take her places. She genuinely loved depending on him; he loved being depended upon. It fed his sense of old-world masculinity — and her sense of marital tradition.

As she would readily admit, she seemed an extension of her husband — a wonderful, loving, vibrant extension, but an extension nonetheless . . . until her husband succumbed in the early-morning hours in a hospital ER, cruelly halting forty years of marriage in one wrenching night.

And it took that soul-shredding tragedy to flesh out the toughness, the gumption, the courage of this woman.

This was a woman who had never before needed to demonstrate such qualities in such quantities before — never had to become her own "I Am Woman" woman until fate forced the issue.

Now in her 70s, this woman who went directly from her parents' home to her marriage home had to learn to be

home alone, crying almost daily. So I asked this woman —
who through seven decades had never lived outside the East
Coast, who fed off the familiarity of her hometown that had
become the substitute anchor in her life — to do the impossible:

Please leave everything you know. Everything that com-
forts you. Everything that anchors you. Even that suspicion
you have that civilized life doesn't really exist beyond the
George Washington Bridge.

Come to Las Vegas.

She did.

"Family," she said, "is the most important thing."

An unmarried woman who still didn't know how to be
unmarried — a stranger in her own life, really — she was
also now a stranger in a new neon land. And she called upon
previously unseen reserves of strength — which she often
doubted she had — to rise above her considerable fears.

Beyond her familial ties — me, her late brother, and his
kidney-shaped pool — she happily found Las Vegas to be a
city suffused with warmth. In the Vegas Towers apartment
complex she moved into on Flamingo Road, near Maryland
Parkway, she was surrounded by neighbors-who-became-
pals from the New York/New Jersey/Connecticut corridor.
As with me, she felt unshackled by any cultural demands
to conform to a lifestyle, an etiquette, a code of interaction.
Vegas told her to be who she was — and do what she had

always done with people she'd always done it with — without an iota of discomfort.

This is a be-who-you-are town. And for a mature woman venturing out of a cloistered domestic life for the first time — and without the partner she always leaned on — that was a perk she wouldn't find most other places. Not in San Antonio. Not in Des Moines. Not in San Francisco. Not in Chattanooga.

I watched, astonished.

At a point when advancing age caused several of her friends back East to restrict or even eliminate their driving, this woman whose husband had often doubled as her driver nervously climbed behind the wheel and, slowly, solo, conquered a new city out West.

While others strenuously avoid the traffic of the Strip, she made a point of driving it at night, taking a childlike delight in its dazzling kaleidoscope of lights.

At a time of life when making new friends becomes a chore and social retreat becomes increasingly ingrained, she barreled ahead, with new friends at her side: shopping at the Boulevard Mall; foreign film nights at UNLV; regular breakfasts at Blueberry Hill diner on Flamingo Road; staring, slack-jawed, at the talking statues at the Forum Shops.

Mom joined a genealogy club, a Yiddish club, Hadassah — family roots and cultural heritage being the foundation of her being.

Though she remained a Bronx girl to her core, she vigorously defended her adopted new home to naysayers, proudly pointing out its positive aspects with a convert's zeal. And she was rewarded with uniquely Vegas moments: Her singing idol, Steve Lawrence — whom I had interviewed and informed of her chaste crush — embraced and kissed her backstage after a show at Caesars Palace (she trembled and felt faint).

East Coast or West Coast, her essence remained: still generous to a fault, thoughtful to the extreme, a Jewish mother forever. ("You're full? First you'll rest — then you'll eat again.")

She passed in 2001 at Sunrise Hospital. And when she died, she took with her the long-overdue respect of an admiring son who belatedly discovered the many layers of a strong, remarkable woman. And gave me renewed affection for the city that helped that happen.

Grateful for that, I thought I could now put to rest my regrets over the one person who never experienced this city's restorative magic. The one who would have embraced it most of all.

I was wrong.

Dad came rushing back to me in another man's story.

Writing for a local magazine, I was assigned to tell a modest dream-come-true story: The newest headliner of the sleek Eastside Lounge at the Wynn Las Vegas was a sixty-something, retired Bronx car repair shop owner. He was discovered singing in a Florida bar by Steve Wynn, who brought him to town and installed him in the resort's cozy performing jewel — a late-in-life success on the Las Vegas Strip.

This was Dad's story, but for the happy Vegas ending.

Both men were born showmen and singers, and responsible, workaday providers. Where they separate is that one peddled booze and bug repellant, while the other tinkered with carburetors and camshafts.

Another difference: One, in a sweet quirk of fate, captured a dream. One, in a sad quirk of life, didn't.

As I watched the former perform — his gregarious charm and mellifluous baritone seducing the crowd as he sang, fronting a trio on a bandstand overlooking the lush, still waters of the softly illuminated pool area — memories of the latter flooded my heart.

In that moment, he could have been Dad's twin. It was in his face — age-lined, but handsome, still flush with the adrenaline rush of performing — and I knew he meant it. Because I knew that look. My dad's look. The one that showed me what joy looked like.

Older patrons in the lounge — plus some younger ones

who gathered at the railing, intrigued by his silky pipes — swayed and snapped fingers to his translations of Sinatra, Dino, Gershwin and Porter favorites my dad could have matched with glee. As he cradled a ballad's finishing notes like delicate china, one woman simply whispered, "Wow."

I whispered, "Yeah, Pop."

Yet a nagging sadness fell over my soul as a memory surfaced, a moment of self-defeatism when my dad wondered aloud why another kid from New Jersey like him — born just two months after him — had become, well, Sinatra. And he hadn't.

Why was destiny so capricious in whom it kissed and whom it slapped?

"I guess," he sighed, "it wasn't meant to happen."

While nowhere near mega-star level, it did happen to this man performing before me, practically channeling Dad. I could see him there, swaying and smiling, as my mind's eye fleetingly treated me again to a warm illusion.

The ex-booze-and-bug-spray salesman was headlining the Eastside Lounge on the Las Vegas Strip.

But no. Dad rests back East, beneath a headstone on which I had inscribed, "Music in His Soul." And I choose to believe that, in a sweet quirk of the afterlife, he is giving an eternal performance, awash in joy.

Still, when I departed the lounge that night, I told this

talented gentleman to cherish his fortune and relish his job — croon it, belt it, sell it, love it. He is performing in a city that can reinvent reality until it's a dream come true.

I did request just one indulgence whenever I returned to see him.

"Forgive me," I told him, "if when I watch you sing solo on the Las Vegas Strip, I hear a duet." ♦

Note: Elements of this essay previously appeared in the Las Vegas Sun *("That's Life: A Mom for All Seasons," May 12, 2000) and* Vegas Seven *magazine ("A Tale of Two Dreamers," November 4, 2014).*

The Current

By Amanda Skenandore
(Fiction)

A shadow rippled behind the window of the boarded-up gas station as they crawled along Highway 95 through Searchlight. That was her first omen.

"We left my brother here once," he said to her with a laugh.

She tore her gaze from the corroded pumps and weathered storefront, looking at him for the first time since they'd left Las Vegas. "At the gas station? Alone?"

"By accident. Thirty minutes before my folks realized and turned around. It was a working store back then." He grinned in that hammy way of his as if to say, *See I'm trying*, and she let the snarky comment about his parents slide back down her windpipe.

Besides, she could imagine it — five yowling children

crammed into his parents' beat-up minivan, pawing at each other with fingers made sticky from peanut butter sandwiches and cherry fruit roll-ups. Easy to miscount heads. And thirty years ago, when the town was just as small but not so dead, what harm could've come to his brother?

She laughed. Mostly for him. So he could see she was trying too. Laughed even as that shadow appeared again behind the busted-up window. When had they last laughed together like this? That cooking mishap on their tenth anniversary? His boss's awkward Christmas party speech four years ago? Certainly long enough not to mind a little shadow.

Several miles beyond, in Laughlin, they checked into their hotel, slipping the clerk a twenty for a room with a floor-to-ceiling river view. They were celebrating, after all. Exactly what, she wasn't sure. A new beginning?

She marveled at their room's renovated interior — the cushy chair and ottoman angled toward the windows, the king-sized bed piled high with pillows, the spa tub and rainfall showerhead. Impressive upgrades for a forty-year-old hotel. He wasn't impressed, though; hurried her out of the room, back into the car, and across the river.

"You're gonna love it," he said when they pulled up to a small dock. "Get out of your head and be one with the river."

He sounded like a rent-by-the-hour life coach. It was only jet skiing, after all.

Her unease mounted as they waded through the frigid

river water and clambered onto their respective machines. And again when he zoomed off, leaving her to flounder in his wake, still trying to figure out how to operate the damn thing. His yellow-bellied jet ski and red life vest became dots of color downriver.

For a time, she'd been adventurous, too. An I'll-try-anything-once kind of girl. When had she become — what had he called her — spine softened and dull?

He came back and idled beside her as she finessed the controls. One thing she could say for him, he always came back.

Together, they turned upriver and raced past the riverfront casinos. Sunlight glinted off the unending rows of tinted windows. Tourists strolled along the river walk, frozen drinks in hand. With the temperature climbing, she welcomed the spray of cold water on her skin.

Not far beyond the casinos, the dam came into view, cordoned off with buoys. *No Trespassing* signs bobbed with the current. They stopped. On the Arizona side sprawled a weedy campground. In college, they'd borrowed a tent from the Outdoor Adventure Club and come down for spring break. Back then, just getting the poles fitted and tent standing felt like an accomplishment. They'd unrolled their sleeping bags and made love atop the slippery nylon shells, the tent aglow with sunlight, its walls shuddering with the breeze off the river.

She leaned sideways on her jet ski and dipped her hand into the water, using her wet fingers to cool the back of her neck. Was he thinking of that trip, too? Of their afternoon together in the tent?

Or of another afternoon?

Another woman?

Perhaps, of nothing at all.

They steered their jet skis around and headed downriver. This time they cut the engines and let the current carry them. Other skiers zipped past, engines aroar, but they were content to drift. They ate sunflower seeds — the cracked-pepper kind he loved — and spit the shells into the water. He regaled her with stories of lizard hunting and boxcar racing, of his first crush and the movie they'd seen together at the casino theater. How thrilling sharing popcorn and holding hands had been at ten years old! He remembered the girl's name — Crystal — but not the movie they'd seen.

"*Beetlejuice* maybe," he said, water lapping at the sides of their jet skis. "Or, what was that movie with Tom Hanks and the giant piano keys?"

"*Big.*"

"Yeah, that was it."

After a moment his smile faded, and he turned away, hiding his gaze in the craggy Arizona horizon. "Heard she's a meth addict now."

It relieved her to imagine Crystal this way — track marks

and rotted teeth — even as she hated herself for it.

His mood seemed to lift as they floated past the Pioneer. Back when he was a boy and his father dealt craps there, the two-story-tall cowboy that leaned against the casino's sign said aloud to passing tourists, "Howdy, folks. Welcome to the Pioneer!" He told her this, and they laughed.

"Guest complained they couldn't sleep with the constant noise, though, so eventually they shut him off."

He told her of the O.K. Corral shootout staged daily in front of the casino, and of the train that ran from the parking lot of the Tropicana to its main door. Except back then it'd been a Ramada Inn.

All this talk about his boyhood enlivened him. He sat straight and easy. He dipped his feet in the river and splashed her playfully.

She didn't mind. Not the splashing or the stories. She'd missed this man, the man she'd met in college, the man she'd married. Never mind none of these happy memories included her.

Once they cleared the *No Wake Zone* in front of Harrah's tiny, manufactured beach, he sped off, calling over his shoulder, "Race you!"

Her jet ski rocked in the sudden chop stirred by his leaving. The engine sputtered as she squeezed the throttle. Then she too was off, her eyes trained on the fleck of red in the distance that was his life vest.

Soon, though, she grew tired of racing. She never won these games, after all. She slowed her jet ski and admired the multistoried houses lining the Arizona shore. Each boasted its own dock and lawn-chair-studded patio. Perhaps they could live there when they retired. Buy jet skis of their own. But this was harder to imagine than his methed-out ex-girlfriend or abandoned brother.

When she tried to coax her jet ski onward, it grumbled and petered out. She squeezed the throttle so hard black rubble flecked off the handlebar. The motor didn't respond. Gasoline choked the air. And he was gone. Not even a speck of red at the horizon.

To her right, on the Nevada side, a towering shell of concrete loomed amid the yucca and creosote. Rebar poles jutted from the top, bleeding rust down the cement siding. Rows of empty holes lined the facade, pockmarks that windows were meant to fill. A lone palm tree stood between the abandoned structure and river. Years' worth dead fronds formed a shaggy skirt about its trunk.

The current dragged her farther downstream. This vantage exposed emerald green graffiti sprawled across one of the building's interior walls several stories up. Otherwise, the concrete was marked only by rust, like a skeleton picked clean.

"That was supposed to be another casino."

She startled at his voice, even though she'd heard the

rumble of the approaching jet ski.

"So far away from the others?" she asked. They were several miles from the cluster of glittering buildings that formed the nucleolus of the town. "What happened?"

"The project was cursed. That was the rumor anyway. Construction men kept dying on the job. Accidents, they thought at first. But when one guy ended up skewered through with rebar, investors pulled out and construction stopped."

She shivered, and he laughed. This time alone. "It's just a dumb rumor. I'm sure whoever owned the place went bankrupt, is all. You're right, anyway. It was stupid to build it so far downriver."

"Why aren't there houses here like on the Arizona side?"

He shrugged.

Maybe no one on the Nevada side could imagine a future alongside this cement wasteland.

She shivered again. "My jet ski's dead."

He boarded her craft and tried to coax the engine alive. Another bloom of gasoline, but no movement. They rummaged around the storage cubbies for rope and tethered the jet skis together.

She rode behind him on his machine to the dock, the way she might have when they were young and only able to afford one ski. The motor groaned if they inched above 15 miles per hour, but she held tight to him, remembering the curve of his spine and warmth of his skin. She wanted to kiss his back, like she'd done so often in their early days, when they'd lain naked in bed together. But his bulky life vest, stained with other renters' sweat, was one more barrier between them.

That afternoon they did not make love. They returned the jet skis and haggled with the owner for a partial refund. Back at their hotel on the Nevada side, he said he wanted to nap, but instead lay awake scrawling through his inane Snapchat feed. She walked down to the neighboring casino and killed time at the Classic Car Museum, even though she'd hadn't the slightest interest in 1929 Ford Roadsters or 1957 Cadillac Convertibles or 1915 Model T's.

They ate a heat-lamp-warmed dinner at the buffet, then battled their fullness with a stroll along the river walk. Raccoons scampered over the rocky banks. A pair of ducks swam in tandem through the marsh weeds. Moonlight undulated on the water's black surface. Despite the moldering fish smell and trash-cluttered shoreline, she found herself enspelled by the town and the childhood stories he continued to tell.

They'd not gone far when a strange, insectile humming rose above his voice. Huge floodlights lined this stretch of walkway, casting the flanking casino in a ghostly glow. Grasshoppers flew in and out of the beams of light. Hundreds of them. Thousands. Like some biblical plague. One buzzed past her ear. Another struck her arm as it scudded toward the light. They littered the concrete walkway, crunching beneath her feet when she didn't watch where she stepped. He clasped her hand, and they escaped into the casino.

They were laughing again, shaking their clothes free of any grasshoppers that had latched on and stolen inside. Chirping slot machines replaced the humming. King-sized chandeliers twinkled from the ceiling. She wiped the soles of her shoes on the worn red carpet, and they wandered amid the aged tourists playing craps and roulette.

"Up here," he said, taking her arm and dragging her up a Titanic-style staircase. "There's an awesome arcade on this level. We used to come with a pocket full of nickels for our birthdays."

But the second story was empty. Haphazard stacks of chairs crowded the corner of a counter-service Mexican restaurant, leaving the dust-covered tables abandoned. The doors of the nearby trattoria were shuttered. The vast buffet at the far end of the corridor lay gutted as a shucked oyster.

She watched his gaze crawl along the bare walls and cordoned off rooms. His boyish smile collapsed.

"Maybe they're just renovating," she said. But she'd never been as good a liar as him. She clasped his hand. "Show me the arcade."

He led her down a short hallway. Black curtains shrouded the mouth of the arcade. Behind the threadbare velvet, an accordion gate blockaded the room. A jumble of old and broken casino equipment pressed against the gate: balding card tables, three-legged chairs, corroded chaffing dishes. A cigarette vending machine stood along the wall, its display cracked. A box overflowing with brightly colored hats and noisemakers labeled *Happy New Year 2010* sat beside it. In the very back, buried beneath more boxes and defunct furniture, was a lone skee-ball machine. Cobwebs tethered it to the wall. Tucked into the corner a few feet away stood an old fortuneteller machine. The mechanized woman caged within leered at them through dust-filmed eyes, her hand hovering above a lusterless glass ball. No other remnants of the arcade remained.

He dropped the curtain. It swished back into place, hiding the bric-a-brac that the casino staff was too lazy to drag to the dumpster. "Let's go."

"Wait." She stood on her toes and kissed him, soft and light. Just enough of a kiss to pull him into the present. His lips were stiff beneath hers. Lifeless. That wasn't unexpected. But then, just as she retreated, he kissed her back. Firm. Fierce. Lively.

He pressed his body against hers, backing her up to the wall. His hands slid beneath her shirt, roamed her skin.

She tensed, turning from his kiss to scan the hall.

"Don't be so vanilla. Nobody's around," he said to her neck and began unbuttoning her pants.

Relax, she commanded herself. Relax. Enjoy this. But she was years out of practice. She closed her eyes, trying to dredge up those feelings from college. When they'd been so hungry and alive. She imagined herself back in the bathroom of the student union when he'd taken her atop the sink, imagined herself astride him in her hand-me-down Subaru in the Monte Carlo parking garage, imagined them twisted together atop the slippery sleeping bags when they'd come here all those years ago with their rented tent.

And she did relax. Their heavy, needful breathing entwined with the silence around them. In that silence, she heard the footfalls of students hurrying to class, the rumble of car engines in and out of the parking garage, the lapping of the river against the campground shore ... and bells. The mechanical kind that chime when you've reached the next level of a game.

She rattled her head to dislodge the intruding sound. But the bells continued, joined now by pings and beeps and laughter. He pulled out of her, unfinished. She opened her eyes.

The black curtain was gone. The metal gate, too. Instead of broken furniture and decade-old party favors, the room beside them was filled with arcade games. Aglow and ringing.

He tucked himself back into his jeans, not with the haste of surprise, but with strange, trance-like movements.

"Look," he said, as if she wasn't already gaping at the apparition. A child's glee infected his voice. He started inside, but she tugged him back.

"Are you crazy? This is ... I don't know. Totally unreal."

"Yeah." He nodded like she'd meant "unreal" in a good way, not a *Nightmare on Elm Street* kind of way. "Come on."

"There's no way I'm going in there."

"But they've got all the classics. Pac-man, Mortal Kombat, Whack-a-mole." He reached into his pocket and pulled out a fistful of nickels that hadn't been there before. "I've got enough for both us."

The lights on the pinball machine blinked and glimmered. Revving engines sounded from the Sega Daytona Racing game. The scent of popcorn and cotton candy permeated the air.

"You promised to try new things this trip. Give us another try." He jangled the nickels. "Come on. I know you love skee-ball."

She glanced to the far end of the room. The net of cobwebs around the skee-ball machine had disappeared. High scores flashed across the top panel in brilliant red.

She stepped toward him. A faint line demarcated the carpet between them. His side new and plush, free of gum stains and cigarette burns. Her side brown and trampled. She took another step.

A light in the far corner beside the bank of skee-ball machines caught her eye. The fortuneteller and her divining ball. The scrim of dust was gone, but her eyes were just as dark and empty as they'd been before. The fortuneteller's arm jerked upright, and in her hand she held a card. Emerald green lettering scrawled across its surface.

She stopped, fighting off a shiver. "This isn't right. Please, let's go."

She held out her hand.

He didn't take it. Instead, he turned and walked with his fistful of nickels into the arcade.

The chirps and beeps and pings were deafening now, raking over her nerves like the metal claw of a toy crane machine. The spinning beacon lights, blinking bulbs, and glowing screens blinded her. Still she lingered, straining to hear his laughter above the din. The fortuneteller in the corner cackled. The buttery popcorn aroma turned to that of rot, like what they'd smelled at the riverside where the water pooled, collecting trash. This time, he wouldn't be coming back.

She ran. Ran through the casino and into the grasshopper-infested night. She ran, not upriver to their hotel, but downriver along the walkway. The towering cowboy tipped his hat to her as she passed. "Howdy! Welcome to the Pioneer." A train whistle sounded from the Ramada Inn across the street.

She ran beyond the glowing edifices of the Golden Nugget and Harrah's into the desert. Sand filled her shoes. Cactuses scratched at her jeans. The brush rustled with animal sounds. Not animals made fat and tame by the careless offerings of tourists, but those still wild and hungry.

In the distance, moonlight glinted off a shimmering

facade of windows. An emerald green sign glittered from the apex of the building where once there'd been only rebar. Grasshoppers swarmed in and out of its light. Neatly trimmed palm trees waved at her from the surrounding lawn.

She slowed and inhaled deeply, even as a chill skittered down her spine. The closer she drew to the building, the brighter the moonlight shone against its facade. Inside, the restaurants and bars and card tables were all alive with people. She hesitated in the marble-tiled foyer. The artificially cooled air prickled her skin. But she couldn't turn back, couldn't brave the darkness and insects and hollow laughter again.

After wandering through a maze of slot machines, she saw a bank of elevators and hurried toward them, skittish of the vacant-eyed gamblers seated before the blinking screens.

She stepped alone into the first elevator that opened. Inside were only two buttons. Up and down. Her hand hovered above them. Down seemed the safest option. Familiar somehow. Inviting.

Before her nerve could fail her, she punched the top bottom. The elevator zipped upward, smoothly at first, then jerking and wheezing. The doors opened to a gaping concrete shell. She leaped out before they could close and the elevator drag her back. Moonlight filtered in through paneless windows. Tall, spray-painted letters sprawled across the far wall. *Welcome to the Emerald River!*

She fell to her knees and wept, grateful for the cold, gritty cement beneath her. Grateful for the moon-softened darkness. Grateful for the silence. But mournful for all she'd left behind. His brother must have cried like this, alone at that gas station in Searchlight. Cried until he'd seen the beat-up minivan chugging back to claim him, then hastily dried his cheeks. She needn't bother to hide her tears. Not anymore. No one was coming for her. Theirs would never be a funny story.

Nevertheless, she stood. No more looking back. A breeze gusted in through the gaping window holes. It smelled only of river. No popcorn or decay. No campfire smoke, or body sweat, or jet ski gasoline. Better that way, she decided, even as she inhaled again, hoping for one last whiff of him. ... Just the emerald river. ♦

Comeback

By Jennifer Battisti
(Poem)

When I was young I ate nuked ravioli in the manufactured
    homes
of the Miracle Mile Trailer Park. Kids in alleyways smiled
with malt-liquor teeth when I stayed out too late. The
    aluminum siding cut
my lips under moonlight while I kissed a boy whose mother
    worked grave-shift keno.
Soon, I was bad karaoke, a cheap steak-and-egg breakfast at
    Slots-A-Fun.
Then, I was stacked glitzy, beveled into a tower,
hoisted by men who tasted like sheetrock.

Vegas economy is a slippery nipple.
The latticed boom, winch and pulley, gypsum made

Comeback

multi-deck dealer's shoe — then, read 'em and weep.
Behind Circus Circus Manor, desert cranes rise and multiply,
the G-string steadied by topless possibility.
Swarovski glints under work boots.
Construction is a choreographed marionette balancing
a 65-ton truss in her twice-a-night smile.
Day shift, the city blisters orange-reflective,
a hard-hat bonanza to punch the clock.
Igloos swing the boulevard in unison, past
the Sands convention center. They wipe
their brows with Dean Martin's cocktail napkin.

Southside, those stadium girls erect
from the cinched corset. The 100-yard-chorus-line
is eclipsed by flight — the future uproar, pom-pom frenzy.
At night, loneliness whips and howls
through their muscular midnight pose.
Sunrise laces the ribcage, warming the new skeleton of
    spectacle,
show-shopper being strung. By noon, the Strip heats
netted legs like hot dice on a bender.
Sharp suits spill martinis on their wrecking balls,
lean over barricades to witness demolition,
reinvention. They ante in bundled explosives,
raise the hushed intermission — that gritty folding of
    concrete.

Jennifer Battisti

I once was an ace of spades in a whirlwind of ash
then resurrected by Jubilee stems can-canning second
    chances
to be an unearthed fuchsia feather fossilized in caliche.
Remake me to dazzle in chinchilla.
Wardrobe-change me into the 25-pound headdress,
the salty olive, curtain closed.
Rebuild me bad odds and carpet, deliberate.
Condense my life, flatten me into souvenir penny,
into a coin I can bite down on for the two-drink-comp.

Boil my heart down into the Mojave electric,
then later, into something people will invest in.
Ready-mix me in the belly of wet potential.
Carve my initials into the gulch.
Make me the dusty bag of old casino chips
reborn under dynamite — a lucky comeback in the rubble of
    the Dunes. ◆

But Also I'm Fine

By Erin Ryan
(Nonfiction)

"SHE'S SINGING WITH A TONGUE REBUILT FROM HER LEG," the title screams, three emojis gaping like some gonzo ellipsis. I want to slap them, to wring adequate shock from their vacant eye holes that Elly Brown is alive, let alone slaying "Amazing Grace" in this video. Viewed millions of times on Facebook alone, it's a potent line in her cancer story.

The forty-one-year-old Las Vegan is telling it to the world through social media, and to me over a lunch she's fighting valiantly to swallow.

"It's hard for me to eat. Sometimes it's a disaster, and I just apologize ahead of time for you having to watch," she says, belting out a laugh like it's a choice she's making.

It's hard for her to even share the thought, given that

her head got taken apart a year ago. A tumor was blooming on the base of her tongue, three centimeters of destructive potential wrapped around a nerve bundle and threatening to invade the jawbone. Stage III. Aggressive. Imminently metastatic.

Since high school, Elly had weathered a patch of wrongness on the left side of her tongue from an inflammatory autoimmune disorder called lichen planus. She learned to avoid triggers like spice and alcohol, but the discomfort became less and less situational. A biopsy revealed a cancerous lump that was removed in early 2017, and she quickly rebounded.

When the pain flared that fall, it was time for a PET scan to root out lurking malignancy.

"It came back clear. So my doctor said, 'It's not cancer. Off to primary care to get some pain medication,'" Elly recalls.

By Christmas, the pain was unmanageable. She went back to her oral surgeon, and this time a biopsy showed advanced cancer. Stunned and scared the diagnosis had been missed, Elly brought her case to UCLA specialist Dr. Elliot Abemayor.

"Here in Nevada, my doctors were talking about debulking the tumor and then finishing with radiation. Dr. Abemayor was like, 'We don't debulk tumors here. We eradicate cancer,'" she says, green eyes lighting way up. "So I found my doctor. He's a total cowboy."

The treatment plan involved a disabling, disfiguring surgery, one Elly had particular reason to fear. She was a professional actress, model, and singer. Catwoman in an indie pilot and random hot chick in Dr. Dre's "Kush" video. Champion of retro lingerie and reliable sedans. Featured vocalist on stages across Las Vegas, international cruise ships, and the stylized streets of a Hong Kong theme park.

She had auditioned for a principal singing role in *Jubilee!* in 2007, when the showgirl spectacular thrived at Bally's on the Strip. Fluff LeCoque, a force in musical theater and the show's longtime manager, listened in the dark as Elly tore into "Don't Cry for Me, Argentina."

And as for fortune, and as for fame
I never invited them in
Though it seemed to the world they were all I desired
They are illusions, they're not the solutions they promised to be
The answer was here all the time

Other contenders had all been cut off mid-song when the panel heard enough, and Elly waited for the ax through the final note.

"Fluff got up from her chair and came over and shook my hand. She said, 'That was so beautiful I didn't want you to stop.' I just melted in a puddle!" Elly squeaks at the memory.

She performed in *Jubilee!* for two years, also landing roles in Holly Madison's *Peepshow* and the Las Vegas Philharmonic's *Broadway a la Carte* between gigs on the cruise-ship circuit.

You can see starkly what she stood to lose scrolling through old posts on social media. Her voice is by turns powerfully rich and perfectly delicate, whether purring through voiceovers or nailing impossible high notes on pop covers. She's a brilliant soloist, but the work Elly loved most was with four-piece a cappella group The Sound Collage. She says when you're layering only human instruments, harmonies can be so pure it changes your cells.

Sizzle reels of her on-camera hosting present a flawless ideal. Her face is all golden ratio, fine bone structure heightened by the creamy skin, full lips, and almost sentient hair of a Disney princess. I can't help asking how she said goodbye leading up to her surgery in May 2018.

"Here and there I thought, maybe I should take some pictures, maybe I should take a video of me singing. And then I was like, no, I have a lifetime of that and I don't want to dwell there," Elly says. This cancer was getting eradicated, even if she had to lose herself.

She trails a finger along the scar running from her left earlobe under the chin and up the lip in a neat zigzag. After making that cut, Dr. Abemayor peeled back her face and removed half of her tongue, part of her jaw, four teeth and all of the lymph nodes on that side of her neck. He worked with plastic surgeon Dr. Irene Kim to rebuild with titanium scaffolding and bone, tissue, and skin taken from Elly's right leg. Tubes were placed in her stomach and windpipe so she'd be able to eat and breathe after so much Frankensteining.

A video she shot after coming through the procedure tells you everything you need to know about Elly. Her severely swollen face makes me think of *Total Recall*, when the heroes tumble into the Martian atmosphere and convulse as the pressure imbalance threatens to taffy-pull and pop their skulls. Yet she gazes impishly into the camera, vocalizing with her mangled tongue earlier than doctors thought possible. Then she pans along her incision and grins. Even here her beauty is intact, in great part because her spirit is.

Another image from her recovery genuinely looks like a movie prop. It's an unvarnished photo of her calf, where parts were harvested for various reconstructions. The wound stretches from ankle to knee, and the thigh graft on top has a bruised, waxy, corpse-like rawness. This side surgery put her in a wheelchair for a month before healing into darkly striated lesions.

Her tracheostomy scar is much more subtle, tucked in the notch where her clavicles meet. A wishbone charm on a gold chain hangs right there, a too-good metaphor for the way loss and luck can muddle. Because Elly does feel lucky.

"I'm really, really grateful," she says, and she's not just talking about surviving. "That's not to say there aren't bad days, and days when I'm pissed off that this happened. I just don't think people take seriously enough how great you can make your life when shitty things happen to you. And shitty things happen all the time! There's treasure everywhere! What if it's our job to be like, *I don't know how right now, but somehow this is better. How could it be better? I'm going to investigate.* When that's where you put your focus, it changes everything. It changes everything you have in your hands, everything you see around you, everything you feel.

"I have to tread so lightly, because I know I'm so blessed and have more resources and support than so many people dealing with problems. But if there were something I could share to help them, it would be that: How to investigate the meaning of this bullshit thing that happened. Let's figure it out. It's amazing when you're just thrown in."

We met in 2016, and I remember thinking that no one could be so constantly sunny, that Elly must be one of those performers who never goes offstage. But the Disney princess thing isn't just about her hair (thinner now, be it from chemo, radiation, or the post-op decision to go from black to platinum). She might actually be flexing when she texts a bicep emoji, just to channel the immensity of her goodwill. She means it, relentlessly. And that goes for seeing the silver lining inside the glass half full.

Take this lunch. I callously ordered Brussels sprouts, not

realizing how daunting they are to someone whose salivary glands were ravaged by thirty rounds of radiation and whose neck muscles haven't mastered compensating for a crippled tongue. Swallowing solid food isn't just difficult, it's dangerous. Elly insists that she relishes the challenge after five months of pumping protein goo into a feeding tube.

Ask about the devastation of her "leg tongue," and she'll tell you how stoked she is to finally be rid of the lichen planus. Some survivors of oral cancer lose the entire tongue, so she sings with abandon through speech impediments that make her sound like she's deaf. Marvel at the uncomfortable tedium she endures draining fluid from her face without lymph nodes, and she'll say it's a luxury having a chin to tend. She even likes the zigzag, so much that she won't get it revised when Dr. Kim smooths out her lip.

"That's my 'I fucking did it' scar. This is where we're at. I'm okay with it."

A recent post on Instagram is tight on her face, showcasing the uneven contour of her jaw and fissure in her smile, dazzling as ever. The caption distills her intense positivity down to an inspirational Rumi quote I want to find corny but can't, because her heart is so visible: "The wound is the place where the light enters you." #scarsarecool

On Facebook, she's been sharing homespun videos like the viral "Amazing Grace" and real-talk insights on cancer-specific issues and others affecting humanity broadly. There are thousands of comments and many private missives from her exploding audience, and she has made it her mission to respond.

Her aim is to inspire and directly support anyone clicking for an ear, an example, a lift, an answer. Nothing about her message is original, she says, but she hopes the delivery helps others find vital information as well as joy in their own messes. She's not trying to fling glitter at those who respond to suffering with justifiable darkness, be it cathartic or toxic. She simply feels enhanced by her trauma, like a superhero born of a radioactive blast, or an alien doing guerilla research on our existential extremes.

That means she's creating from a very different place. On her YouTube channel, old offerings range from defending popstar Fergie's crucifixion of the national anthem to asking tourists on Fremont Street about animals' fashion preferences. (Spoiler: Foxes love leggings.) Two videos of her self-care routine contrast then and now. The one from three years ago is a cheerful PSA on making your own exfoliant soap to avoid those offending plastic microbeads. The one from this March is a funny, fascinating tutorial on treating scars and lymphedema with special tape, rollers, compression garments, pumps, and, and, and. "When I used to think about starting a YouTube channel, I wanted to talk about fashion, beauty, handbags maybe. That's cool. Let's talk about my face vibrator," Elly deadpans in the introduction.

Head and neck cancers constitute a deeply lonely disease, she tells me. Occurrences are rare, so there's no pink-ribbon equivalent. Sufferers have to dig for community. Even when they find it, there is a need for more Virgils guiding newbies through hell with research and recipes, commiseration and strength.

Elly Brown found her niche. Just in time for her doctors to find another cancer.

"I'm sitting in the parking lot, and the call comes in. I knew. My doctor felt really bad about having to say it over the phone, but so much has happened, and that day was so weird and raw anyway there really wasn't anything she could say in that moment that was going to destroy me," Elly says of being told she has breast cancer.

It was mid-April, and she was in Florida helping with her father's funeral. She had just come from viewing his body.

Michael Brown's pancreatic cancer diagnosis came right after Elly scheduled her surgery at UCLA, and she'd been visiting every couple of months and FaceTiming every other day. Her fiancé gave him an Oculus Go virtual-reality headset, trying to keep the world open even as Michael's life got very small. He didn't have the chance to wander inside photographs. The decline was just too fast.

His wife, Caroline, was the only one there when he stepped both feet into the Kingdom. In his delirium he kept saying, "Oh boy. Oh wow." She asked if it was beautiful, and he said yes.

Elly buried her daddy's ashes in a tree-filled cemetery in his hometown of Sunbury, Pennsylvania, down the road from her childhood home. She and her sister and two brothers sang at the memorial. "When the River Meets the Sea" was her idea, a sweet ballad from the 1977 Jim Henson TV special *Emmet Otter's Jug-Band Christmas*.

We are born and born again most gracefully
Thus the winds of time will take us
With a sure and steady hand
When the river meets the sea

Patience my brother and patience my son
In that sweet and final hour
Truth and justice will be done

Like a baby when it is sleeping
In its loving mother's arms
What a newborn baby dreams is a mystery

But his life will find a purpose
And in time he'll understand
When the river meets the sea
When the river meets the almighty sea

Before he died, I asked Elly if she ever fell apart over what she faced in cancer's wake, and she said no. Watching her dad fold up, confused and hurting — that's when she lost it.

One of their things was bingeing on Turner Classic Movies, especially the musicals with sprawling sets and epic dance numbers, *Brigadoon* to *Guys and Dolls*. He never tired of being her wingman in these decadent escapes.

"My dad was a man of few words," Elly says when I ask if they had *that* conversation, when a parent knows he's leaving his child. "He said to me once, 'You know, honey, you're my role model in all of this.' And I think he was trying to tell me in his way that he was really, really proud of me and that he hoped he could be as peaceful about everything."

That flashed in her head as she absorbed the news about the mass in her right breast, the same cancer her mother fought at age forty-seven. Given the grim odds with that family history, and the fact that Elly remains on the knife-edge of oral cancer recurrence, she embraced "taking a sledgehammer to an ant." The plan was bilateral mastectomy, despite the rogue tissue being confined to a tiny cluster of calcifications inside a single milk duct.

She needed to know she wouldn't die from breast cancer, to feel that solidness like stone under quicksand. But the need dissolved into the realization that no amount of cutting could separate her from the specter of the larger illness, from always holding her breath.

Beyond that, every specialist she consulted favored a less drastic approach, bolstered by tests showing no known links to breast cancer in Elly's genes. If a lumpectomy doesn't do the trick, however, she is resolved to let another part of herself be reinvented. It helps that she sees powerful stuff in her existing scars, and that her Instagram following does too.

She says she doesn't miss her old body.

"The way that we look at books for wisdom or spiritual leaders for meaning, they're just signs that are pointing to something. And my old body was beautiful; there was nothing wrong with it. But now when I look at myself, it's pointing to something so ... just bigger than me, so much more awesome, so much more interesting. It means so much to me, and I want everyone to feel that feeling. It really makes me sad to think that people would want to hide that, because in that is this profound pointer arrow, you know? Like a sign or indication that there's so much more going on than we could possibly imagine, and it's wonderful.

"I'm open to the fact that it could be more like a computer simulation than the picture we like to paint of God and heaven. I think that God is everywhere, in everything, in every cell, and every bit of matter. I think there's a connection, and when we open ourselves up to it, we feel it more. Wherever you put your focus or your expectation, it comes. And I don't think that's a magic thing, like a weird hippie woo-woo thing; I think that is very much logical. It appeals more to the analytical part of my brain than my creative brain. It's just everywhere, pouring out of everything, and when I'm really listening, I feel peace that I can only describe as the Holy Spirit. I feel that it's very much accessible to us, and when I call on that power, whatever form it's really taking, it's there. And I've never really fallen. I've never not been caught and given something to help.

"In our moments of pain, when it's the hardest to look for that, those are the moments when we can find it the easiest. It's almost like it comes closer to us but we just don't see."

In the land of Mennonites and Shoofly Pie, a six-year-old Elly discovered the stage. Her sister was performing in the high school's production of *The King and I*, and kids were needed. "From that moment on, anytime I was in a theater I was like, this is where I belong; this is my home; these are my people."

Opportunities to explore the arts were limited in Montgomery, a blue-collar gas stop along Pennsylvania's Susquehanna River. But in and out of church, the Browns were a musical family. They lived modestly, Dad a manager at a women's prison and Mom a nurse at the Catholic hospital, yet there was always room for the piano lessons Elly hated.

Walking the block to school every day for thirteen years, she dreamed of being in the bustle of a grand showroom, whether dancing in the hot lights or working miracles behind the curtain. But she never took dance. Her exceptional voice carried her to a degree in musical theater from West Chester University.

While her parents warned against pursuing an artist's life, having watched their older daughter scrape, they never said no.

Obviously, Elly moved to New York City.

"I lived in this Dominican neighborhood at 191st and St. Nicholas, and my subway stop was right next to a fish market that stuuuuuunk. Hot summer days were the worst. All the fire hydrants were broken. All the ladies would be watching their kids play in the street, sitting on the stoops talking to each other," Elly remembers. "The men, whenever they would see me in the street, they would just say, 'God bless you, God bless you, God bless you.'"

If He did, it wasn't in the form of the acting jobs she hunted so fiercely. She was serving beer and nachos across from Central Park, barely paying rent and waiting for something to give.

At twenty-two, she took herself to the Southern Theatre Conference and did a blanket audition. Her voice was
the ticket to a six-month contract on the Costa Victoria, a
cruise ship bound for Europe. It kicked off a six-year run on
floating stages, doing Broadway, Latin classics, knockoffs of
Cirque du Soleil. Elly was a company manager and a married
woman by age twenty-eight, when she moved to Las Vegas
and joined *Jubilee!*

Her husband was a dancer from Hungary, and he struggled to find his place in the Strip's incredibly competitive
entertainment scene. Tension built, and Elly thought returning to sea might fix whatever was wrong. Instead, her husband fell in love with someone else.

"I look back, and I think he really did us both a favor,
because I would not have left," she says. "He really broke
it hard, but it was good. My life got so much fuller because
there was space then for real things to happen. Ricky wouldn't
have given me the time of day if I was married when I met
him."

She can't remember exactly how they became friends
on Facebook, but Elly says a photo of Rick Lax on a toilet
got her interested in her soon-to-be husband. Technically,
he was above the toilet, fully clothed and using a laptop. It
was the cover of his third book, about being a stunt journalist in Vegas. She looked through his pictures and conjured a
charming identity for this writer/magician/lawyer who clearly

was smart and full of hustle. After commenting on an image, she got a message from Rick asking how he knew her.

She was bouncing between work in Las Vegas and home in Southern California at the time, so they met for lunch in Hollywood. He took her hand as they strolled and gave her a paper rose she figured he'd made a hundred times before. "I was enamored with him," she says.

Over the past five years they fell for each other, moved in together, and became dog parents and creative partners.

Rick, whose portfolio of Facebook pages boasts millions of followers and more than a billion video views, was in the business of making viral content. "I did a video for Ricky about having people guess what vegetable I was thinking about, and that stupid video … it got like forty-two million views," Elly says, warmly.

She was moved to produce her own content, knowing "pretty white girl" wasn't a niche but never settling on a theme or message that resonated far beyond her existing circle.

Getting sick changed that. In the year since her surgery, The Elly Brown Show page racked up more than 200,000 followers, and the episodic posts typically have six- to seven-figure engagement.

"I have a niche now. Didn't ask for it, didn't want it, but I have it. So am I going to throw that opportunity away? Or am I going to work really hard at making something valuable that could actually help people that's not just, 'ten handbags you need right now!'" she says, adding that she watches those handbag features all the time. "When I started making these videos and getting a good response, there was a shadow in my head saying, maybe if I heal too well too fast people won't listen anymore. That's crazy! I have to get well to show other people they can get well. This is an evolution."

Her audience on Instagram just spiked above 10,000, coinciding with a shout-out from famed Paralympian, TV star, bestselling author, and Las Vegas native, Amy Purdy. Elly is focused on leveraging such momentum, but her reach is potentially way beyond social media. She is working as a public speaker, her first three bookings with the local library system, an international restaurant group, and a rodeo event in Louisiana for which she'll give a keynote and sing the national anthem. She is wading into oral cancer advocacy, running her own informal awareness campaign and driving significant traffic to forums and support organizations. She's guesting on podcasts and not-so-secretly writing a book.

Maybe someday, she muses, she'll have the celebrity-burnished platform of a regular on a hit show. For now, it's enough to think about the future of *Rise of the Catwoman*, a fan film for which she starred in the first chapter not long before her surgery. As the titular superhero, she won a 2018 Maverick Movie Award for Best Actress in a Web Series. The creators are game to shape the Batman mythology around Elly's new reality. She's thrilled, even knowing how insanely risky it would be dodging a villain's punch with a reconstructed jaw.

"I was frustrated after I won that award. And then I thought, fuck it, there was an actor on "Breaking Bad" with cerebral palsy. If I abandon acting, then I abandon it. And if I don't, then I play characters where there's room for that, and it's my choice," she says.

If it's the former, the irony will be that the sheltered small-town girl is now working with a serious vault of pain to reference. If it's the latter, she'll be able to apply her acting teacher's advice on a new level: If you're a hot dog and they want a burger, you'll never be right for it. So work on being the best hot dog ever. When that's the dish, you're at the top of the list.

In nine hours over five days of going through painfully fine details of being shaken by cancer in every way imaginable, Elly cries only once.

She's explaining the change in her voice. Before treatment, she had such command over the muscles in her mouth, over her breath, that music flew from her. Damaged now, her own flesh fights her impulses. Everything is brittle and weary. What felt like freedom has become "walking uphill with two bags of groceries that are about to burst."

And no matter how much energy she pours in, she doesn't sound like herself. Her range is lower, her tone hollower. She lisps. Some of this will improve with time and surgical revisions, but Elly may never feel it again, the soaring.

"I'm trying to work through this with my therapist, because sometimes I think I haven't devoted enough time to really thinking about what happened to me and what I lost. Here it comes," she says, laughing her way into tears. "And I have to do that, because my mind is so good at protecting me and saying, well you might have lost that but check out this thing over here, this shiny thing that's awesome that you could do! And I'm like, yeah, that seems good, I'll do that. I've never felt hopeless because I see a path, seagulls that say the shore is near. There are choirs for people who've had laryngectomies, if you can believe it. There's a way to keep music in my life. I haven't entirely discovered how that works in, but I know that I will."

It's the certainty of shore that makes Elly different. I ask if she's read about the brain of world-class rock climber Alex Honnold, who famously scaled El Capitan's three-thousand-foot sheer cliff without ropes. Scans showed that his amygdala doesn't respond to fear like the same region in normal humans, and I wonder if Elly is from his planet.

She's aware of her otherness here and understanding when loved ones need her to comfort them about her condition. Rick has gone through as much emotional trauma as she has physical, she observes. He had to get over being afraid to touch her.

He posted recently about a scare they had, when doctors found pulmonary nodules in Elly's lungs, where oral cancer often spreads. The situation resolved, but it pushed them to be in the moment profoundly. "We started to imagine what it would be like if there were just a year or two left," he wrote. "And now the goal has to be to figure out how to live like that — like time is limited. Cause it is, right?"

We know the answer, yet Elly moves in ways that defy it. She's taking time to let things unfold instead of having a "cancer wedding." She thinks she and Rick and their dog Bodhi will live in Las Vegas for five more years before picking a new spot to conquer. She has embryos frozen and a starring role to land, and countless people to help from Tennessee to India.

I imagine the gorgeous swirl of that future as I pause the "Kush" video fifty seconds in. An elevator door just opened on the untouched left side of Elly's face. She is frozen behind Dr. Dre, perfectly in profile, eyes hidden behind huge sunglasses. No smile, despite the party raging. This is her playing a part, manifesting someone else's vision. It's what she did before.

In the video for indie-pop artist Kezar's "Don't Touch the Queen," Elly is Elly. She luxuriates in her fluid-pumping vest and rolls her scars, struts around with Bodhi and with

Hen Friend, the stuffed chicken Rick had Dr. Kim adorn
with matching sutures.

Don't touch the queen
That crown is gold
Don't touch the queen
Can't be controlled

She dances with other badass women, all survivors of
something. And she walks forward, fire in her hands, absolutely ready. ◆

Shared Secret

By A.D. Hopkins
(Fiction)

Carson parallel-parked his Mustang in the last available space near his friend's house in Paradise Palms. He locked the door carefully; something he had learned to do routinely in Las Vegas, even in a good neighborhood such as this one. The car was eight years old now, but he had promised himself a '68 Mustang if he got home alive, and had kept the promise. Anyway, used cars were the norm in his new profession. He had parked in a two-hour zone though he expected to remain longer; the sticker identifying him as a *Las Vegas Sun* staff member would protect him from a ticket.

Journalism hadn't been Carson's first career, but he felt lucky to start a second one. Several of his classmates had spent their entire adult lives in their chosen profession and were permanently assigned to Arlington. There, even a Silver

Star didn't advance one's career, especially if awarded posthumously.

He hadn't even liked journalists when he'd met them in-country. They always asked discomfiting questions, such as what was to be gained for the loss of so many lives, American and Viet Cong and those of non-combatants caught in the crossfire.

"Above my pay grade," Carson had answered the few times he'd been asked that. Now he wished he had asked it himself, before an operation began. Being a very junior officer, he had always assumed somebody higher up had a really good reason. Remembering that reminded him of a motto widely spoken in his new profession: "'Assume' makes an 'ass' of 'u' and 'me.'" He intended to live by that, as he had once lived by patriotic mottos.

He tried to push melancholy thoughts aside as he entered his friend's property. He was here to celebrate Michael's success, rather than to regret his own mistakes and his country's.

"Talk about journalism," he told himself. "Talk about movies. Sports, maybe even literature. No war, no politics."

The house was a single-story with a roof that came to a peak over an entryway higher than it needed to be for the double doors, as if two slabs of roof had fallen against one another. One of the windows in the front of the house was round. To Carson it suggested the Flintstones lived there, but the residents were actually Michael and Bess, who had purchased it when Michael was promoted to pit boss. They had bought it from the man he had replaced, who also had been promoted and was therefore able to afford an even-more-fashionable neighborhood.

The party was in the backyard, and Carson entered by a gate between the house and a free-standing garage. The garage was wide enough for two cars but Michael's new sports car, and Bess's station wagon, were parked on the driveway in front of the garage. He didn't see the third-hand Jeep that Michael had driven when he toiled for the newspaper before taking a casino job.

In the backyard, women swam in a pool and lounged beside it, some wearing the tiniest bikinis Carson had ever seen. One seemed unaware she wore no top to her bikini. All the women were slender and fit, reminding Carson that Bess had been a dancer in the *Lido de Paris* show at the Stardust Hotel. Now she did public relations and placed advertising for such shows, but the pretty women might be friends who were still dancers. All the men watching the women were fully dressed, in expensive casual clothes and well-shined shoes. Those were probably husbands, or Michael's friends in casino management. Carson reminded himself to ask, rather than assume either.

Michael called to him from the patio outside the kitchen

door. Wearing a barbecue apron over his slacks, Michael was a muscular man, about forty, who still had a thick head of dark, expensively trimmed hair. Carson, five years younger, was beginning to lose his. Michael pointed at a small portable bar near the pool. "Hard liquor at the bar. Beer and wine in the ice chest. Have all you want; tell me if it runs low and I'll get more out of the refrigerator in my studio."

Michael was grilling steaks. Carson knew prime beef when he saw it, though he had not seen any since college days, when he held a summer job at a swanky restaurant. Prime beef was unavailable in Las Vegas markets because hotel gourmet rooms monopolized the supply, and most residents could buy it only stolen, and sold, by a hotel employee.

Carson tried not to ogle the nearly naked women at the pool as he fished in the nearby ice chest. He selected a Japanese beer he had learned to like on the far side of the world. He strolled across a lawn smooth as a golf green, to stand beside Michael.

"Go inside and look around," Michael said. "I hung my best photos."

"You still shooting?" Carson asked.

"You bet I am," Michael said. "The way I dreamed of all those years. People offer me more gigs than I can handle, so I just shoot the ones I really want to. I make money at it, but I don't have to; the casino pays my bills. I built my own studio and darkroom in the garage; it's got better equipment than they had for the whole staff when I worked at the paper."

So that was why the cars weren't in the garage. It was no longer a garage, but a studio. Michael was his best friend, but Carson felt a small stab of discomfort in his chest and recognized it as envy. Michael was living his longtime dream, by practicing his art without compromise, in a state-of-the art studio he personally owned. Carson's dream had been a distinguished military career, and though he didn't want it anymore, he hadn't found one to replace it.

Carson went into the house to look at Michael's photos. They were enlarged and matted in poster-sized, silver-colored frames, spaced at equal distances from one another along a hallway, where Michael had installed gallery lighting.

"They're great, aren't they?"

Carson turned to see the speaker. She was the most appealing woman he had ever seen, a slender beauty with hair the color of a red fox, green eyes, fair skin, and small, perfect white teeth showing when she smiled. She had dimples at the ends of a wide, expressive mouth, wore very red lipstick, and no other makeup Carson could see. She wore a lime-green mini-sundress covering an ample chest, its hem above the knee but even so a little longer than it had to be in 1976. She wore no stockings on this hot spring day; and flat sandals of green leather.

"Err, yeah," Carson stammered. "He's the best photographer I ever knew."

"How do you know him?" the beauty asked.

"We worked together at the *Las Vegas Sun*," Carson explained. "And you?"

"His wife and I are close, so Bess got him to shoot my portfolio a few years ago," she said. "This is me." She pointed at a framed photo of a show dancer in a costume rich with real ostrich feathers and possibly real breasts, swelling charmingly from a jeweled and sequined bra. Despite her attractive coloring, the photo was black and white; Carson remembered the photo from a newspaper ad for a show at a Strip casino. He mentioned where he had seen it.

"Closest I ever came to fame," she said, laughing. The laugh sounded like treble notes on a good piano.

Strolling side by side they came to a photo of a man's hands, dangling loosely from a small window, the window frame and sill blackened with smoke. The photo was a vertical, perfectly proportioned and naturally lighted from the side. Carson remembered the day Michael had shot it, with the late-afternoon sun low in the west and the smell of burned carpet and burned flesh rising from the ruins of a mobile home.

"That's a disturbing picture," she said.

"It's the reason Michael quit photojournalism," Carson said. He was bitter about it, but the beauty's direct gaze and interest made him spill the story. Besides being perfectly composed and poignant, the photo told an important story.

Mobile homes that could not pass inspections in other states could be sold legally in Nevada, and were. Some of them caught fire and sometimes people died in those fires.

The photo was dummied into a front-page layout until an order came from the publisher's office not to run it anywhere in the newspaper. "It's too gruesome," was the stated reason.

"I think the real reason was that the ad director didn't want to lose any advertising from mobile home dealers," Carson said. "So the newspaper kept those ads, but the Legislature hasn't fixed the law and they still dump third-rate mobile homes in Nevada, people still die because of it, and the best photographer we had left us to work in a casino."

"That's horrible," she said. "What does that title mean? 'Mans Morts?'" She mispronounced the term. Carson corrected her.

"Mains Mortes," he said. "It's French for 'Dead Hands.'"

The picture, beautiful and terrible at the same time, held her gaze and Carson could tell it bothered her. It was supposed to do that. Apparently to fill the awkward silence, she asked, "Have you lived in France?"

Carson answered, "No, but I spent some time where a lot of folks spoke it." Once he said that, he realized it pointed toward a subject he wished to avoid, and tried to think of some plausible lie about how he knew French.

"Vietnam?" she guessed.

Carson gave in and admitted it.

"If you learned French, you were probably an officer," she guessed. "West Point?"

"VMI. That's Virginia Military Institute. It's a Southern version of The Point. VMI sent its cadet corps into battle in the Civil War, and some of 'em got killed. They were just boys, but for some reason we used to be proud of that!" He wished he never had been proud of it, and didn't understand himself why he admitted he once had.

"Are you still a soldier?" she asked.

"No and never will be again. Now I cover crime news for the *Sun*. The beginner's beat."

"With a background as an officer I would think they'd put you a little higher up," she said.

Carson couldn't explain that for every American who appreciated his service, another blamed him for a lost war or starting an unnecessary one. As if anybody had asked his opinion! Her remark angered him, so he struck back.

"A woman who looks as good as you do in a green dress could probably get a job with her clothes on," he observed.

He expected her to turn away at the insult, but all it did was bring out the musical laughter again.

"I had to start over too," she said. She extended her hand. "My name is Janet."

Carson told her his name and asked how she had started over.

"I used to be a ballerina," she explained. "But I was too

tall to get lead parts. That's the story for most of the women here. We start training when we're little girls, and nobody knows which ones are going to stay petite, which is what they want in ballet. The ones who grow too tall have to go out for basketball, or come to Las Vegas."

Carson was tall himself, and hadn't noticed that Janet looked directly into his eyes, though wearing sandals without heels. He realized she was nearly six feet tall.

"So you became a showgirl?"

She was offended. "Don't ever call a dancer a showgirl! All showgirls do is look pretty wearing a tall headdress and not much else. There aren't many showgirls anymore. I'm a dancer, and that means I have to know how to dance, and I get to keep my boobs covered."

Carson laughed now. "Guess I had that snarl coming. But thanks for explaining the difference."

Her anger seemed to pass as quickly as his own had. Carson liked that in people.

He said the only ballet he had ever seen was the previous Christmas, a Nevada Dance Theater production of *The Nutcracker*.

"I was in it!" she exclaimed. "I was a shepherdess!"

Carson was delighted to remember her. "The only one with red hair! You said were too tall for ballet!"

She said, "Too tall for leading parts, but all of us lanky ladies try for the minor ones. That's why the Nevada Dance

Theater is so good; everybody who gets any part at all can dance as well as the lead!"

"That's a good situation," Carson said "Being able to keep up your art while doing something to pay the bills."

She replied, "Looks like that's what Michael's doing. I want him to update my portfolio but he hasn't found the time yet. All us dancers want him to photograph us, but he's so busy I don't know anyone who actually got him to do it."

They were standing close together, still looking at pictures, though Carson found none he had not already admired back when Michael worked at the newspaper. He had hoped to see some of Michael's new work.

"Hey, my beer's empty," Janet said. "Will you split another with me? I can't afford the calories in an entire one."

Carson liked the idea of drinking from a bottle that had touched such pretty lips. So they went into the backyard and found the ice chest. She wanted a particular German beer, but none of those remained.

Carson remembered, "Michael said there was plenty more beer in the garage — or I guess I should say his studio. Do you think he'd mind if we went in there and got a few bottles?" He and Janet both looked around for Michael or Bess, but both were engaged in animated conversation with another attractive couple.

"They're having fun," Janet said. "They probably won't mind if we help ourselves."

The garage's side door was not locked. A refrigerator hummed in the darkness, and Carson located it by sound, planning to get an armload of bottles to resupply the ice chest. He felt for the door, opened it, and light flooded the garage.

"Oh, hell!" Janet said.

"What's the matter?" Carson asked.

He turned, expecting to meet her eyes, but instead of at him, she was looking deep into the garage interior. At the far end, dimly lit from the refrigerator door, a workbench stood with what looked like a photo enlarger, an Army poncho draped over it for a dust cover.

Developing sinks were filled with what looked like auto parts. On one wall hung pull-down rolls of backdrop cloth, but in the foreground where a subject would be positioned for photography, Michael's old Jeep, its hood propped open and its tires flat, occupied the floor space. Both Jeep and studio were no longer works in progress, but works abandoned.

"He's not taking pictures!" Janet surmised.

Neither Janet nor Carson touched the beer in the refrigerator, nor spoke another word until Carson closed the refrigerator door and darkness again swallowed the room.

"We never saw this," Carson said then.

"Yes," Janet said quietly, her voice musical in the darkness. "It's very important we *never* tell anyone."

And it became a secret bonding between them, something they knew about Michael that he had purposely kept from them despite long and loyal friendship. Sometimes they mentioned it to one another in bed, remembering how they had met. Once Janet mentioned it while delirious with a fever their first child had brought home from kindergarten. But they never told anyone else what they had seen, and most of all, they never told Michael. ♦

The 'Managed Metamorphosis': Oscar Goodman and the Transformation of Las Vegas

By Steven Sebelius
(Nonfiction)

Oscar Goodman didn't buy a new pair of eyeglasses when he was elected mayor of Las Vegas. But suddenly, the city he saw through those glasses looked very different.

Where before he saw a perfectly fine downtown business district, suitable for lawyers and bankers and real estate professionals during the day, he now saw decay and neglect. In his words, he began seeing the "little weeds" choking off the city's progress.

Las Vegas — most particularly the downtown part of Las Vegas — was badly in need of new business, new development, a new life that would save the core of the city and reverberate out into its far-flung neighborhoods.

It needed reinvention. And in the person of Goodman — a longtime criminal defense lawyer turned unlikely politician — it would get it.

But first, Goodman needed to reinvent himself.

It wasn't the first time Goodman had considered giving up law for public life. He'd mulled a run for mayor before, in 1995, against then-incumbent Jan Jones. But he'd opted out, telling the *Las Vegas Review-Journal* at the time that "I would have been the world's worst mayor. If I would have won the race, I would have hated the job. I just can't kiss people's rear ends."

Four years later, Goodman had apparently changed his mind, or at least looked at the seat differently once Jones opted not to seek another term. On March 6, 1999, the very last day to file for municipal offices, Goodman held a news conference in the atrium of his law office on Fourth Street. He literally stood behind a copy of the U.S. Constitution, declaring his candidacy. Law partner David Z. Chesnoff had suggested framing his career not as a mob lawyer, but as a protector of the constitutional rights we all enjoy. And Goodman ran with the idea.

"The juices are flowing," Goodman said, according to the *Review-Journal*'s Mike Zapler. "I've never done anything in my life other than to win it. I am dead serious and there is no joking around."

At least one of his opponents, then-Las Vegas Councilman Arnie Adamsen, sounded like he needed to be convinced: "You've got to be kidding me," Adamsen told Zapler. "This is great. I love it. The more the merrier."

It was no joke. Still, behind the announcement was a serious hurdle for Goodman to overcome. For decades, he was the man standing beside alleged mobsters, in court and out. His waiting room was like a barber shop for goodfellas, always full of nicknamed associates of a mob that Goodman often denied even existed. He was associated with people such as Philip Leonetti, Nicodemo Scarfo, Meyer Lansky, Anthony Civella, Frank Rosenthal and — most of all — Tony "The Ant" Spilotro, the alleged murderer who himself was beaten to death and buried in an Indiana cornfield.

And now he wanted to be — in his own words — "Las Vegas's ambassador to the rest of the world"?

The city was immediately skeptical. He was dubbed the "barrister to butchers" in an editorial in the *Review-Journal* titled "Anybody but Oscar" that ran four days after Goodman's announcement. "And as the most visible personification of the 'new' Las Vegas, he'd be a PR catastrophe," the editorialists said. A second swipe during the campaign asked whether Goodman was "the phantom menace" and concluded, "How Mr. Goodman will reflect on Las Vegas in a national debate on gaming [regulation] is not a 'phantom menace.' It's a real concern worth considering before Election Day."

Goodman's candidacy came at a time when Las Vegas was trying gamely to reinvent itself, not as the sin-drenched adult playground where alcohol flowed more freely than the valley's scarce water, but as a place for the whole family. Treasure Island — with a nightly pirate show more akin to Disneyland than Las Vegas — had debuted in 1993, the same year the MGM Grand Adventures amusement park opened behind the eponymous casino. It was to be a short-lived, even half-hearted stab at luring family visitors, but the contrast between Goodman (who represented a darker and more bloody era of Las Vegas history) and the "new" Las Vegas was stark.

How was Goodman going to pull it off? First, he didn't shy from his past: "I'm proud of the work I've done my whole life," Goodman said, according to Zapler's *Review-Journal* account. "I've represented people by upholding the United States Constitution."

After a campaign that grew nasty at times — Goodman was pilloried for comments he'd made critical of Megan's Law on a television point-counterpoint show — Goodman made it into the runoff with Adamsen. The two people could not have been more different, with Adamsen dubbing himself "Mr. Crossing Guard" and Goodman not shying from his love of gambling and drink.

In the end, the "new" Las Vegas decided it preferred the

"old" Las Vegas as a leader: Goodman won the June 8, 1999, runoff 64 percent to 34 percent. It would be the closest race of his 12-year mayoral career.

Goodman said he wasn't concerned during his run. He easily raised money, and he campaigned — even in the Las Vegas heat — in his traditional pin-striped, double-breasted suits. In court, he said, he had to look jurors in the eye and be believed, "or else I was done," he said. On the campaign trail, it was much the same. "If somebody looks you in the eye and shakes your hand, you've got their vote," he said. "I knew I was going to win."

But for Goodman — who claims he never even knew where City Hall was until he went there to file his candidacy papers — victory was a jumping-off point. "I didn't know what you were supposed to do [as mayor]," he said. "I followed my instinct."

Something about Goodman's brash indifference had captured the public's attention. He embraced, rather than ran from, what he called his "former life" as a mob attorney. He extolled the close ties between the mob and Las Vegas. Goodman liked to say that when people visited the city and kicked over a rock, they wanted to see a little Tony Spilotro, not a little Mickey Mouse. And, as he told *Las Vegas CityLife* shortly after his election in 1999, "If I was a podiatrist, they wouldn't be writing about me at all."

Early stumbles

Goodman's reinvention got off to a slow start. He gave an interview to reporter Connie Bruck, writing in *The New Yorker*, in which he reveled — Donald Trump-like — in the reaction that he got from the public. ("They love me!" he said, a quote that became the headline of the piece.) But he sounded very much like one of his old clients when he told Bruck he was keeping a list of those who opposed his candidacy for mayor "as though I were the Antichrist." On the list: Then *Review-Journal* publisher Sherm Frederick. When Bruck observed that Goodman sounded like one of his former clients, he responded like one: "Well, why let your enemies survive?"

The interview led to another story in the *Review-Journal*, one in which he said Bruck took him out of context and failed to recognize his brand of humor. "She took me very literally," he said, again, sounding like the future President Trump. Another editorial followed, a sort of told-you-so lecture encouraging the mayor to call his former clients "sociopathic scum" and distance himself from what they represented.

But Goodman never did. He stayed loyal to his former clients, even as he sought to grow into a new role representing his newest and now only client: the city of Las Vegas.

"Everything is role playing," said Goodman, known for his courtroom dramatics and out-of-court statements, such as declaring it was better to murder than to be a rat, or that he'd rather his only daughter date a mobster than an FBI agent. But now, in his new job, he acknowledged, "everything is different."

One of the things that changed: his approach to the media. "It taught me a lesson, I'll tell you that," he told *Las Vegas CityLife*, speaking of *The New Yorker* interview. "I'm going to be very slow about talking to people who don't live in Las Vegas."

Goodman's reinvention had begun.

Transforming the city

Goodman said he knew to truly transform Las Vegas would take a lot more than getting a few new bars downtown, and slapping a new coat of paint on the aging downtown casinos. To truly reinvent Las Vegas, to make it a world-class city, Goodman would need to make major changes.

His list, which did not change over 12 years in the center seat at City Hall: Bring major-league sports to town. Bring arts and culture to town. And improve the sorry state of the city's medical sector, which inspired one of Las Vegas' most cynical jokes: Where do you go when you get sick in Las Vegas? The airport.

Unburdened by the restrictions of municipal government, or the conventions that governed regular politicians, Goodman was able to reinvent the job around his particular skills and personality. A natural with a gift for gab, Goodman began calling on people such as the commissioner of the National Basketball Association, or the owner of the Oakland Raiders (long before Las Vegas Sands CEO Sheldon Adelson put a deal in motion to bring the Raiders to Las Vegas). He met with the CEO of the Rouse Company, then a shopping mall and community developer.

Some ideas never came to fruition, but many others did. A block-long river running between Las Vegas Boulevard and Fourth Street, dubbed, of course, "Oscar's River." A reinvented Fifth Street School as an arts and culture hub.

And then there was one of Goodman's other signature achievements, undertaken with the usual controversy: Reinventing an old post office and courthouse (one where Goodman himself had argued cases) into a museum chronicling Las Vegas's mob history. The idea came early in Goodman's tenure, with the attendant criticism of him for allegedly glorifying the mob. But Goodman stuck with the idea and brought about what we know today as the Mob Museum, the National Museum of Organized Crime and Law Enforcement. On the museum's original board of directors: a former special agent in charge of the Las Vegas FBI office.

All these things were part of Goodman's slow-but-steady transformation of the city.

The seeds of the city's transformation weren't far from where Goodman had come to work every day on Stewart Avenue. Just down the street — and literally on the other side of the Union Pacific railroad tracks — was a vast, undeveloped parcel of land that had been envisioned as the site of everything from a domed football stadium to a park.

Goodman wanted the land, and he began negotiating. Although Las Vegas is technically a strong-manager form of government — in which the mayor and city council set broad policy, but the city manager runs things day to day — Goodman's outsized personality drove the reinvention he wanted to see. But if he held sway over a compliant bureaucracy, he had more trouble with people outside City Hall.

"A lot of what I did, you couldn't do without the private sector," he said.

That was a hard-learned lesson, however. Goodman was a frequent and early critic of Las Vegas' business community, calling casino companies, bankers and developers out for a lack of "altruism," a synonym for failing to support Goodman's agenda of revitalization, including projects such as a performing arts center and a sports arena downtown. The same Goodman who earlier said he didn't like kissing people's rear-ends had little trouble kicking them, and in that he was unique in Las Vegas politics.

But ultimately, even Goodman realized he could catch more flies with honey. Speaking on a gambling industry-sponsored TV show in 2002, Goodman made a pseudo-apology to the industry. "I understand how important it is, as the mayor, on behalf of the citizens of Las Vegas, that I get along with the most important industry, the driver of our economic well-being," he said. "I understand — and I've matured in this job — that you can't do everything by yourself . ... We need the gamers because they are, in fact, they are the IBM, the U.S. Steel, as far as Nevada is concerned.

"That's one of the reasons I'm here today because I've learned a lesson," he added. "I can't — and I say 'I' — the city can't accomplish these objectives [an academic medical center and a professional sports stadium] without having the support of gaming."

Goodman the lawyer — in what Bruck had dubbed in the 1999 *New Yorker* piece a "managed metamorphosis" — was swiftly becoming Goodman the politician.

Goodman's relationship with the private sector allowed him to do something that many consider the centerpiece of his 12 years in office: acquiring that 61-acre parcel of vacant downtown land. After the deal was announced in October 2000 (the city gave up 99 acres in a northwest technology park and $2 million in cash), Goodman began, in his own formulation, playing monopoly.

And just like the board game, Goodman began changing the face of the city.

Because of him, the World Market Center built a mammoth furniture showcase adjacent to the city's 61 acres. A thriving outlet mall broke ground across the street in July 2002. A longtime friend of liquor distributor Lou Ruvo, Goodman got a medical center studying Alzheimer's and similar diseases located downtown, in a building designed by world-renowned architect Frank Gehry. (As Goodman tells it, the undulating design of the building came from a crumpled up piece of crepe paper that Gehry tossed around his studio during their initial meeting.)

And the jewel of downtown development, the Smith Center for the Performing Arts, grew out of travels that Goodman took with community leaders Don Snyder and Myron Martin. After a visit to the Kravis Performing Arts Center in West Palm Beach, Florida, Goodman recalls saying, "We need one of these." And Las Vegas got one, although it wasn't an easy lift.

Goodman also credited his relentless salesmanship of Las Vegas for a burst of downtown high-rise residential projects, including the Juhl, the Ogden and the SoHo Lofts.

"I sat up there and I pontificated," said Goodman, who made sure to meet with the press weekly and "accidentally" let slip details of pending projects, thus ensuring interest in Las Vegas and its offerings remained high. He was particularly proud of a *New York Times* story that labeled the 61 acres "the jewel of the desert," believing it started phones ringing at City Hall like never before, with developers and media alike.

Goodman, in many ways, foreshadowed Donald Trump before Trump took on the national stage. He often excoriated the press, even while courting reporters with his weekly news conferences. In one 2001 interview, Goodman told interviewer Julie Albertson that he had "very little respect" for most local reporters, whom he called "little eels that slide back and forth from reporters to commentators" and that "they write half-truths, that they're mean-spirited and that they're not what I consider to be professionals."

In another infamous incident, he threatened to bar a *Review-Journal* reporter from City Hall for asking questions about a 1999 meeting with Charles "The Moose" Panarella, regarding a job for Panarella's son.

He *didn't* say "fake news," which would not come into vogue for another 18 years or so.

Much like the real president, Goodman made a point to hold a "State of the City" speech each year. The first year, the speech was held in the modest theater of the since-shuttered Reed Whipple Cultural Arts Center, with the city staff, council and Goodman marching in like cabinet members to the real State of the Union. By the time Goodman's time in office was over, his speech took place high above downtown in the World Market Center, with floor-to-ceiling views of a skyline literally transformed by his efforts.

He's the mayor now

Goodman's tenure as mayor did come with some philosophical changes, too: The man who traveled the country challenging the government's power and authority grew frustrated with the limits of his own power.

Goodman's approach to the homeless was a frequent source of criticism, and earned the city the moniker of meanest to the homeless in August 2003. He saw the problem — which stubbornly persists to this day — as an impediment to redeveloping the downtown. He criticized other local governments for doing too little to help with the problem. He once suggested housing the homeless in the distant, shuttered prison in Jean, and expressed surprise when people objected to the idea of literally putting the homeless in jail, even a jail where the doors wouldn't be locked. (On the other hand, when he signed on as the celebrity pitchman for Bombay Sapphire, he donated half of his $100,000 fee to homeless services.)

Goodman's tirades against graffiti taggers was legendary: The one-time civil rights crusader suggested cutting off their thumbs after a decorative desert tortoise placed in a revamped Spaghetti Bowl was defaced. He later suggested putting them in the stocks for public humiliation.

And Goodman's administration sparked many free-speech battles over the Fremont Street Experience, as solicitors pestered tourists under the lighted canopy, and the city waged war with ordinances and lawsuits to stop them. Asked why he'd take a pro-government position so opposite from the one he took for decades as a criminal defense attorney, Goodman had a simple reply: He was the mayor now.

"Oscar's the mayor now," he said in December 2002. "As a lawyer, I was just concerned that my clients weren't being prosecuted unlawfully. Oscar Goodman the mayor wants to see downtown thrive. This is an area that's been blighted by cockroaches. ... In the past, nobody bothered them. Now, we're bothering them. I don't know any other way."

There were other stumbles, too. In 2005, Goodman was speaking to a third-grade class when he was asked by one of the pupils what one item he'd take with him to a desert island. Goodman infamously replied, "a bottle of gin."

Given his penchant for the substance — Goodman has been the pitchman for Bombay Sapphire for years and is definitely brand-loyal — it's probably a good thing he didn't say "A case of gin." But the comment still went viral, a throwback to that fateful *New Yorker* interview.

And Goodman responded in much the same way, not by apologizing, but by citing his essential honesty. "What I've learned from the experience, in certain venues, perhaps you can't answer the question. I will not lie, when I give an answer. I'm not going to say I'm going to bring a teddy bear to the island, or I'm going to bring the Bible to the island. I'm not going to lie to anybody because that's not Oscar Goodman. But sometimes, you can't tell the truth because of the people with whom you're speaking."

Asked in the news conference if he had a drinking problem, Goodman had a classic, unrepentant reply: "No. Absolutely not. I love to drink." And when confronted by the *Las Vegas Sun* about his remark, he replied that he could not tell a lie. "I'm the George Washington of mayors," he said, without irony.

Reinvention

That incident with the third-graders shows unmistakably one truth about Oscar Goodman, the lawyer, the mayor, the man. Unlike the city he represented for so long — and make no mistake, Goodman was the face of all of Las Vegas, even and perhaps especially those parts that lay outside city limits — the reinvention of Oscar Goodman is perhaps one of the biggest Las Vegas myths of all.

Las Vegas, in fact, has reinvented itself many times over: Dusty railroad stop to frontier town. Sin City for workers on the Boulder Dam. Gambling mecca in the desert. Sawdust floors to carpet joints. Megaresorts. Family-friendly destination to What Happens Here Stays Here. Nightclub hotspot.

Business and convention destination. Foodie mecca. And the list will go on.

But Goodman? He only appeared to transform himself from mob lawyer to politician. In truth, Goodman didn't change very much at all.

The same bombast Goodman used in the courtroom (and for the cameras assembled outside) he used from the City Council dais. The same techniques he used to persuade juries he used later on developers, with the same kind of success. The same pinstriped suit-wearing, martini-swilling lawyer who saved so many accused mobsters from their federal pursuers is the same pinstriped suit-wearing, martini-swilling mayor who strides through casinos and courthouses reveling in the attention, telling associates he could not lose a case, or a political race, no matter what office he chose.

The same successes that made Goodman the go-to lawyer for those accused of the most heinous crimes in Nevada and nationwide made him the voters' go-to choice over three terms in office, two of which he won with no less than 84 percent of the vote. Had term limits not intervened, in fact, Goodman may still be mayor today. (In a way, he is: Goodman's wife, Carolyn, won three terms in her own right, and may have her third term extended by a year because of a switch of municipal elections to even-year cycles. If that happens, a person named Goodman will have been mayor of Las Vegas for 25 years straight.)

The same Goodman who avoided federal scrutiny and FBI handcuffs as an attorney avoided the pitfalls of having to answer to the whims of his donors, because of his independent wealth built up over a career in the law. The one major scandal of the Goodman era did not involve doing favors for big donors; rather, he was accused — and found guilty, and later acquitted — of using his title and resources to try to help his son.

It's a supreme irony, then, that Goodman was able to transform an entire city's skyline by simply being himself, relying on his personality, his force of will and his instincts. Politics may change people, but Goodman changed the office more than it ever changed him. Goodman's predecessor, Jan Jones Blackhurst, may have been the first "celebrity" mayor, but Goodman took the office to new heights, and ruined Las Vegas for a boring, crossing-guard elected leader ever again. And while he still evokes comparisons to President Trump, Goodman was always more savvy and more effective at accomplishing his goals.

Remember Goodman's list, the things he believed the city needed to become world-class?

Professional sports: Las Vegas is now home to a successful major-league hockey team, and soon an NFL franchise, even if both are located in the county and not the city. (In fact, long before Bill Foley proposed hockey in the T-Mobile Arena, Goodman envisioned a hockey arena downtown.)

Carolyn Goodman is pushing for a Major League Soccer team to locate in downtown, so sports in the city may yet come to pass.

Arts and culture: Patrons regularly see Broadway shows and musical performances in the Smith Center for the Performing Arts.

Medicine: The Lou Ruvo Cleveland Clinic Center for Brain Health has been treating patients for years, and the Las Vegas Medical District soon will be home to the UNLV School of Medicine.

Downtown: A part of the city that closed up at 5 p.m. now rings with new bars, restaurants, a thriving arts scene, even an independent bookstore.

About the only thing Goodman didn't get in his tenure — or see come to fruition in the years afterward — was his oft-repeated idea to bring a fixed guideway to downtown. His idea — first expressed in his original State of the City address — to extend the monorail south from its terminus at the SLS-nee-Sahara never materialized, thanks more to the monorail's constant financial problems than to a lack of acumen on Goodman's part. (He even once testified before Congress to try to get funding for the downtown extension of the monorail.)

Even if Oscar Goodman hardly changed at all, the city he led for 12 years was reinvented.

Epilogue

As he contemplated the end of his tenure in April 2011, Goodman revealed he was meeting with the Las Vegas Convention and Visitors Authority about the prospects of a job. In many ways, the position would be similar to his official, elected role, minus the ministerial duties of presiding over council meetings and attending official events.

Convention leaders wanted Goodman to act as a brand ambassador for Las Vegas, welcoming conventions to town in a way only the former mob-lawyer-turned-mayor could, with a martini in hand and showgirls on both arms.

"I'll only consider it if it's a serious job," Goodman said at the time. "I'm not going to become a caricature of myself in my next life."

No need. The Oscar Goodman Las Vegas transformed around is fine just the way he is, and always was. ◆

Attention Reinvention

By Harry R. Fagel
(Poem)

Riding hard in the dark nights of Las Vegas
Scoping out the street with keen vision and
Fierce intent
Clocking for the clockers
Preying on the predator
Looking for trouble
Praying for trouble
Finding it every night
Man beats wife, wife beats kid, kid steals from store,
    jaywalks across the street hit by car driven by drunk driver,
    fired from work, angry as hell he
Plans and plots
Shoots the place up and on it goes
Every human tragedy out on the asphalt quilt

Spelled out in the predicate crimes
Rape, murder, theft and debauchery
Symbols of our darker humanity
Drugs and desire sold along with guns and hellfire
Every night out in the Vegas bake
Cop for 25 years out here
Sucking it up
Blowing it out
Keeping it cool
Risking it all
Front seat witness to death in all its inglorious;
Suicide, homicide, abuse, neglect
Trying to keep blood off your boots when it's up to your neck
Screams of grief echo every time but you turn the sound
    down and
DO YOUR JOB
Spit on by idealists
Revered by purists
Dissected by journalists and
You keep marching on
Going up the ranks
Responsible for more and more and more
People, places, things
The phone rings
Forever
Sleep is a barely remembered luxury

Reserved for the normal and the sane
Pressure building and building
News reels and cheap thrills as
Killers roam high school halls and
Celebrities hang themselves in expensive hotel bathroom
    stalls
Being a police officer is akin to stepping out of a plane at
20,000 feet and completing complex tasks as the
Ground screams closer
Every day, even on vacation, the scenarios
Screen by the eyes
Memories and tactics swirling and whirling
Boiling and ultimately
Keeping you alive
Back to the wall in restaurants
Guns hidden where you can grab 'em quick
Questioning loved ones like suspects and all the time
Being a little better than the rest because you
DO YOUR JOB
Suddenly
Rip cord pulled
Inches from the hard-packed earth
I retire
Feet gently touching down but Lord did I feel the g-force in
My aching heart and back
Sudden silence

No ringing phone no
Lives at risk no
Worry to the exponential
Only a quiet moment stretching
Stretching out only broken by
Birdsong and wonder
Such a quiet place
Distinct and real
No screaming victims no
Active shooters no
Hate-filled diatribe only
Potential
Pausing and feeling the cause of a moment's peace being a
Quarter century of risk and struggle
Looking for trouble out on the street
A memory instead of a daily routine
Focused now on all the beauty
I played a part in keeping
Safe ◆

Rewrite

By Mike Prevatt
(Nonfiction)

Should I stay or should I go?

It was June. Just a few weeks left to grab lunch or coffee with friends. We'd meet at our usual meeting spot on campus: a sloped, well-manicured lawn that was seemingly impervious to student wear and tear. And all the friends spoke excitedly about their very-certain futures — their summer internships, their forthcoming European travels, their future grad school, their target wedding dates.

"What about you?"

I was contemplating a fifth year — not because I needed the credits, but because I had zero plans and umpteen regrets.

My undergrad rap sheet: Half-ignored syllabi. Woeful party attendance record. Two student jobs and a schedule as swollen as my diabetic grandmother. Five-figure debt. Two classes that took three quarters each to complete. A crippling gastrointestinal ailment beyond the comprehension of the Top 10 medical school that guess-diagnosed it (treatment: "stress reduction"). An equally crippling depression, nourished by a steady diet of Radiohead's *OK Computer*.

And no girlfriend. Clearly I needed to stay on another year because *this* time, I'd make the necessary eye contact and unforced small talk to land my future wife.

Either I came to my senses or took a rare look at my checkbook, because I chose going over staying. I tossed my mortarboard cap alongside my friends — and the guy who played Samwise Gamgee in *The Lord of the Rings*, who could afford every pencil on campus but still needed to borrow one of mine every lecture — and began strategizing my adulthood.

I also began to obsess about Las Vegas.

I loved Las Vegas. It was in the blood; my parents took me as a teenager and I continued the tradition as a college student. Dismissive of budgetary restrictions, I visited numerous times with friends old and new, thanks to the Strip thrift of yore and a laughably conservative gambling regimen. I couldn't afford many undergraduate rites of passage, but I could plunk down for a 21st birthday in Vegas. Any excuse I could dream up was enough to call my travel agent (aka my friend's mom), pack up a duffel bag, and motor to the Mojave.

One of those visits involved a music conference, which I covered as a student journalist. At that point, I had yet to give serious consideration to becoming a professional music writer. Music reigned over my life, and opining about it was a rare joy, but it wasn't gonna score me a pad in Santa Monica. And yet, during that trip, as I bounced from panel to stage, scribbling notes and meeting contacts, I began to wonder if my future was staring back at me from the reporter's notebook — and maybe from the neon that surrounded me.

Back in Los Angeles, I shelved my summer away working at the campus bookstore, where I argued with co-workers about the appropriate section for *Fear and Loathing in Las Vegas* and pondered my life and how deeply unsatisfied I was with it. I had managed to become both insufferably sensitive and self-flagellating. I shuddered at the thought of reporting on L.A.'s music scene, one rich in editorial possibilities but intimidating in its sprawl and poisoned by The Industry. And I was sexually frustrated, as one becomes when one lacks the confidence to approach potential partners — and certainly when one is convinced those potential partners should be Gender X, but his nighttime fantasies and porn intake involve Gender Y, ultimately dulling whatever attraction one stubbornly believes one has for Gender X.

My life had become a terrible Morrissey song. (I even had a composition book full of terrible Morrissey-inspired poetry to prove it.) But at least I was self-aware. Denial, fear, and inertia could neither blur nor stop the persistent mental scroll that things had to change — drastically.

So, somewhere between my weekly re-alphabetization of the entire fiction section and concert-cramming before my college press pass expired, I sent off résumés and clips to four different Las Vegas print publications and called all the Vegas musicians I'd met at EAT'M who had talked up their nascent scene. I wrote pro-and-con lists for staying in Los Angeles and going to Las Vegas.

And then, in early September, just before the panic could settle, I heard back from one of the alternative weeklies. That was all I needed to start packing. For dejection to turn into enthusiasm. To believe that I might change my life if I changed the skyline in my window. To exploit Las Vegas as so many others had: as a promised land where I could liberate myself in anonymity. For the second time that summer, I chose to go.

Las Vegas lost its mystique right after my arrival, starting with video poker. Jesus Christ, you could not escape it. I so much as needed a Coke and there it was, often played by chain-smoking burnouts in faded Sam's Town jackets. The omnipresent slot machinery singlehandedly dissuaded me from gambling, to the relief of my anemic bank account.

Then there was the Strip. A lack of funds also meant limited options on the Boulevard, once my playground and now someone else's. I relocated just in time for a resort boom. The Bellagio was days away from opening, with Mandalay Bay, Paris, and The Venetian close behind it. But what did the post-family-bait casinos offer someone awaiting his first student loan bill?

Beyond the Strip, Vegas felt alienating, dusty, and colorless. Even the franchises I had patronized in Southern California — the Barnes and Nobles, the Chili's, the Targets — felt unfamiliar and uninviting. I assumed the worst of anyone who didn't smile at or acknowledge me. Rich folks from Beverly Hills could dismiss me all they wanted, but I wasn't gonna tolerate the same sniffiness from the cashier at Port of Subs. And once I did get to know a few folks, they tended to flake out of plans. Socializing in general was a struggle. My new internship meant I was spoiled with comp tickets to any number of concerts and shows. Apparently everyone else was, too.

My bad attitude probably wasn't served by my new residence: a Budget Suites off Paradise Road, which sat adjacent to a crime-ridden neighborhood.

I'd come to Las Vegas for change. To take control of my life. To shake my funk. But this was not the direction I needed to take — quite the opposite. Was that more despondency I felt in my gut, or just the usual excess bile? Didn't matter, and Pepcid was no match for either.

Fortunately, a previous visit had me discovering Cafe Enigma, a downtown coffeehouse that often featured poetry readings, musicians, and people who looked like they hadn't given up on life yet. I declared it my future hang, and hang I did immediately after my move, usually holding court on its porch and, if I was lucky, joined by one of the few people in town I knew.

Like the local musician who helped talk me into relocating. Ron met me one evening and welcomed me into the city. I responded by inviting him to what would become my first Vegas concert (and maybe the worst: a Gary Cherone-led Van Halen at the Joint). And after I told him about my living quarters, he invited me to live with him and his friends. Desperate for residency, companionship, a consistent internet connection, and some semblance of normalcy from whereupon I could tackle all that was stymying my existence, I immediately accepted.

We found a corner-lot house southeast of the Huntridge neighborhood. There was space. There was a pool. There was a garage Ron's band could use for rehearsals. And there was Clay, our burly diva of a roommate.

Within weeks, Clay had asserted habitational dominance by autocratic fiat despite my name next to his on the lease. He was granted mother-hen status by the other musician-roommate, Taylor, the world's most passive guitarist, and their mutual friend Damian, who only seemed to shower for special occasions. Clay decorated all the common areas of the house before anyone else could contribute, most prized among all his adornments being a human skull — likely to keep surveillance over the occupants when Clay himself could not. And when the Queen saw something he did not like, or was challenged for a unilateral decision he made, he let you know about it, temper habanero-hot, with insults and even threats. Upon receiving my note asking him to please not throw away my boxes without asking me first, he warned me of a beatdown should I question his judgment again, and called me a whore for good measure. Little did he know that I actually aspired to whoredom — as, for that matter, did Clay, an overweight gay man who took over-the-counter diet pills with the goal of finally leaving Gipsy nightclub with a man on his arm. Still, his inner turmoil only ratcheted up the tension he stirred up inside our home, which often left me doubled over with nausea.

Perhaps worst of all, Clay gave me a terrible impression of Vegas homosexuals. I knew better than to assume he represented all homos, but his embodiment of every negative gay stereotype did my internal homophobia no favors. Even when I finally came clean with myself that I was at the very least bisexual, I decided to keep that shit to myself inside Casa de Clay. Not only did I not want him to know I was queer, but there was no way I was playing for any team that could also claim him, or so my twisted logic compelled me to feel.

He wasn't the only one padlocking the closet door. Here I had been granted a job covering bands, but as cultural timing would have it, nu-metal and rap-rock bands dominated both the charts and the Vegas music scene. Those shows were always a crapshoot, not just in the variance of awfulness exhibited during the performances, but in how many times a singer or someone in the crowd might use the word "fag." In fact, I could be at the mall, or waiting for a movie to start inside a theater, or just taking a piss in a public bathroom, and I'd hear some asshole drop an F-bomb — never in my direction, praise be, but it didn't make a difference. Even at work, I could not escape the toxicity. One of the louder reporters declared anything that he didn't like as "gay." To wit: The name Mandalay Bay? "More like Mandalay GAY!" he boomed. No matter how much I trusted the other staffers, no matter how much I wanted to clear the air about why I never brought a date to our off-the-clock hangs, there was no way I was sharing my personal business lest it open me up for ridicule.

Then again, what would I have told them? That I fantasized about men every time I shook hands with the governor, but had sexual dreams about women in my sleep? That I dated my friends' female co-workers, but ended each interlude with an awkward hug? That I cruised the mall looking for good-looking dudes, knowing full well I wouldn't approach them anyway? I had no easy explainer for where I was on my psychological timeline.

Grasping at any sliver of heterosexuality, I was skewering my sexual development — and that, too, was tearing up my stomach. As such, my depression returned, kicking and screaming. It didn't matter that one of my goals, to find employment as a music writer, had already come to fruition, complete with all the shows and CDs I wanted. The other three frustrations I vowed to tackle and overcome — my undefined sexuality, my qualmish gut, and my unremarkable social life — seemed worsened by the move to Vegas. Homesickness surfaced earlier than I expected; I racked up phone charges talking to any L.A. friend with the time to hear me whine. I felt alone, despite being surrounded by people more often than not.

I needed a breakthrough. And I got one — at Club Utopia.

When electronic music thump-thump-thumped the mainstream in 1997, I was ready. I was raised on Depeche Mode and the Pet Shop Boys, fell for New Order right around puberty, grooved in my bedroom to England's acid house and Madchester scenes in high school, and — humblebrag — raged to Prodigy well before "Firestarter" set MTV ablaze in 1996.

The so-called electronica movement in the States meant a flood of music through the channels by which I received music. So I began building a critical pedigree outside of rock. Reviewed everything within the genre — literally everything. Requested interviews for anyone who would talk to a college student. Saw any performance with a drum machine: the Crystal Method, the Chemical Brothers, Orbital — everyone except DJs. I wanted concerts, not clubs. The former were meant for watching; the latter, dancing and social engagement — not ideal for a campus wallflower.

My electronic music obsession continued at the Vegas alt-weekly, encouraged by my guitar-worshipping editor who wanted nowhere near that shit. But I was unfulfilled in the live performance department because the dance acts generally passed over Las Vegas. So I braved the rave scene, where I cautiously roamed among people who danced, made eye-contact and even introduced themselves, as if everyone was a potential friend. Whatever — music dork here just wanted to hear something more underground.

Apparently there were additional spaces for that. Like Liquid 303, a vinyl shop for DJs and dance music enthusiasts. Enthused, I checked it out and — lacking a turntable — decided to buy a DJ mixtape. Wore it out, went back and decided to buy another by the same DJ. Turned out the same DJ was working the counter, whereupon I showered him with embarrassingly effusive praise.

"Have you been to Utopia yet?" he asked.

"Are you trying to sell me Ecstasy?" I asked.

"No. Club Utopia," he said.

"I've only been to the Indiana Jones club inside Luxor," I said.

"Utopia isn't in a casino," he said. "Come Saturday night and check out my live DJ set."

Hmmm. I had friends coming to town, expecting to Vegas it up. This would do. "Put me down plus-two," I said, already possessing the freebie entitlement of a Las Vegan.

Club Utopia, as I'd soon find out, was the most revered dance club in Las Vegas. The Strip party palaces were for tourists, cliquey types, and people who wanted to get down to songs they already knew. Utopia was for the real dance music heads — the fans who were underserved elsewhere in the city, the ravers who graduated from the warehouses and four-walled movie theaters, the scenesters looking to establish some credibility, queers like me who couldn't hang with Britney Spears remixes at Gipsy and Freezone, and everyone else with an open mind. At the time, Utopia was the only place in Vegas that could lure the world's greatest DJs into coming to Vegas. And when those DJs closed up their vinyl cases, you headed straight for the upstairs patio, where joyous, beautiful house music boomed until the sun was overhead. It was as close to paradise as the Strip got.

I shudder to think how I might've dressed up for my virginal visit, or how I likely approached the doorman with the declaration that I was on the DJ's list, or how I probably complained about bottled water being five dollars. And I'm sure we looked like total newbs once we stepped on the dance floor for the first time. But within minutes, I was awash in goosepimples and dancing with abandon to pounding four/four beats, blissed out by euphoric synth melodies. I soon forgot that my friends were nearby as I closed my eyes and swam in arpeggiated synth lines, my feet as carefree as they've ever been, my smile from ear to ear.

When I opened my eyes, I noticed that some of my fellow dancers had moved into the three elevated dance cages. One boasted two girls, dancing close enough to tease the dudes below them but rendering their physical contact with a no-homo subtlety. Another contained a single beautiful woman whose fluid, intuitive moves suggested she was a pro.

And then there was the one farthest from the DJ booth but closest to our little circle, occupied by a dude. He looked like the brand of UNLV beefcake that Abercrombie & Fitch would park at the door to welcome shoppers, with the same khaki cargo pants but minus the bulging polo shirt. I successfully turned our circle sixty degrees so I was directly facing him. He had perfectly defined abs and pecs, pencil-eraser nipples, and a groomed but sweaty treasure trail below his belly button. That alone set him apart from the guys on the dance floor — as did his moves. Dude flung his hips and booty in every direction, synced perfectly to the pulse of the PA. He struck his glistening arms out with the choreographed assurance of a cheerleader. And he'd occasionally squat down and thrust his crotch in a grinding circular motion, as if he was working the bachelorette suite at Bally's. At one point, he reached for the button atop his cargos, unfastened it, and slowly moved his zipper down the length of his crotch, exposing his white briefs. I was as fixated on homeboy as a pitbull on a mailman. And worse than the full stare on my face was the full salute in my pants. For the next ten minutes, I tried any way I could to obscure the tenting of my own cargos, cursing my choice of boxers that night. Only after he halted his gyrations and jumped out of the cage did my Judy Blume moment end. I knew better than to follow him. But I wanted to.

I returned to Club Utopia a week later, and again and again, fueled by my passion for its soundtrack, my insatiable urge to dance, my hope that more attractive fellas would also be there — and that I might work up the guts to approach them. I was not only initiated into a sanctuary of sensorial escape and sexual anticipation, but into the greater world of nightlife. It would give me a new work beat that I could exclusively (if briefly) own, eventually expand my social opportunities beyond my musician friends, and grant me a long-overdue confidence boost. What seemed terrifying just a year ago now felt liberating and revelatory.

My budding homosexuality now sparked, I became more open to male/male opportunity, however it presented itself. I went from cruising online personals to crafting one of my own, answering every response, no matter how ridiculous or depraved it was. I happened upon a fully nude male strip club in an industrial area of Henderson, and got my first private lap dance. I would allow myself to become smitten by certain gay male characters on TV (mostly from MTV's *The Real World*). And despite a longstanding discomfort with massage-like sensations, I allowed a friend who was training to be a masseur to practice on me, and my revulsion toward physical touch vanished after ninety heavenly minutes.

All this might have propelled me into proper gaydom had one thing not been nagging at me: God. Though I hadn't been a practicing Catholic since I was fourteen — when our church suddenly kicked my siblings and I out of catechism, just as they'd excommunicated my parents on absurd grounds a few years earlier — I struggled to shake the word and ways of my apparent maker. I couldn't find the happy medium between being myself and becoming some sort of religious ideal. And I obsessed about the notion of homosexuality being a sin. As such, I was wracked with guilt every time I snuck a look at some passing guy, every time I looked at porn or pleasured myself, every time I imagined a scenario where I lived happily ever after with a man. Convincing myself I was bisexual wasn't just a cowardly cop-out — it was my last hope for salvation.

Luckily, somewhere in 1999, my sexuality now a wild stallion I could not tame, I took a hard second look at religion — be it through things I was raised with, things I'd picked up and read along the way, even visiting a Christian church with a friend who insisted Jesus was my homie. But once I rode the logic train through my spiritual terrain, I surmised that if there was indeed a God, he could not have put me on this planet to sustain a lifelong facade of heterosexuality, or that he would cast me into hell (if that existed as well) for acting upon the very sexuality he bestowed upon me. Why would a benevolent, loving God do that to me and my LGBT brothers and sisters, and not the other ninety percent of people? Add all the other natural questions about faith, religion, and God's existence, and I decided that deep down, none of it computed, and wrestling with it made no sense. Until something else compelling *and* logical presented itself to me, I would reject the arbitrary mandates and social constructs of organized religion, and the irrelevant traditions of my past. I would accept agnosticism — and myself as a gay man.

This realization came at a perfect time, because I got a response to my personal ad from someone also named Mike. After some back and forth, I asked him to a Tori Amos concert at the then-new Mandalay Bay, and he accepted. This began a series of outings that didn't carry the pressure of dates, but felt more special than just friendly hangouts — at least for me.

I would find out later that Mike had a non-cancerous tumor in his neck, which was doing a number on his thyroid. He told me this in response to a late-night, poorly conceived email I had sent him where I spilled my feelings for him. But my first genuine crush, the first boy I'd come close to actually dating, was in no condition for romance. He had to go back to his hometown in New Jersey and undergo a procedure during winter break. He softened the blow, though, in two ways: telling me that patience might reward both of us, and inviting me to stay with him during the turn of the millennium — which meant New Year's weekend in New York City.

Having such a great time over those five days only made what happened next feel that much worse: Mike disappeared and never re-engaged with me. I know now that he officially left Las Vegas that January, and that he survived his health scare. But at the time, the episode caused my first dose of heartache and triggered a ferocious bout of depression.

I did the only thing I could do at that point: cycle through every downer album I owned, and throw myself into my work. And it paid off, as my criticism improved discernibly and my future as a music journalist seemed cemented. I also found a local digestive disorder clinic and got a legitimate diagnosis for my class-IV stomach churn: gallbladder disease. As soon as I got back from the East Coast, I underwent surgery. Three weeks later, I was able to eat nearly anything I wanted, and I could now partake in alcoholic beverages. That culinary bacchanalia was tempered somewhat by my underlying irritable bowel syndrome — it's always something, isn't it? — but I considered my long gastrointestinal tempest abated. By March or April 2000, I felt like I was living large in Las Vegas. But I still longed for companionship, and the more I dwelled on it, the more I wondered if I had a greater chance of finding it back home.

Before my trip and surgery, I'd scored an iMac from my folks — a bigger-than-usual holiday gift. This meant easier access to, well, everything, including whatever gay shit I was pursuing online. A site like gay.com would seem so obvious, so generic-sounding, that I almost didn't investigate. But besides all its articles on how to introduce a third person into your relationship or argue with your homophobic uncle, the real value of gay.com was its chat function. I had been warned about the carnality of AOL's discussion rooms, so I figured I'd try these other ones — maybe there was more substantial conversation going on. Maybe I could suss out who was actual boyfriend material. Maybe someone whose interests overlapped my own might peruse my online profile, open up a private window, and reach out. I naively put all my hope in this cyber-fantasy; it seemed considerably less anxiety-stoking than going to a gay bar and interrupting someone from his video poker to stoke conversation.

My first date was four years younger than me and thus unable to enter a bar, but that didn't matter. We went out for Italian food, and on the way to the Fruit Loop gay nightlife district, stopped by my house so I could get something. He used the opportunity to initiate a back rub. Needless to say, we didn't make it to the Fruit Loop, and I had my first sexual encounter in Las Vegas.

This began a succession of hook-ups and dates — none of them warranting a second go-round, mind you, and some of them faring poorly. And then, a glimmer of hope: Johnny, who saw my profile, opened a private window, and introduced himself with a hi and a picture. Dude was hot — hotter than I had been accustomed to. We quickly transitioned to the phone and set up a date, which, like the Italian dinner date, led to the removal of our clothes pretty swiftly. This time, there would be a second date. And a third. Had we hit pay dirt?

More like caliche. After the initial, superficial conversations that bookended movie outings and bedroom romps, what started to surface was *no bueno*. Johnny had very pedestrian tastes in, well, everything. He was also very Christian; his mammoth Ford pickup bore a praying Calvin (from *Calvin & Hobbes*). Which meant he was deeply closeted — as in, no one but me knew. Friend introductions would be tough. When one finally happened, he introduced himself as by a different name. I thought he was giving my pal a pseudonym. But later, at a dinner with his family at Black Angus steakhouse in Henderson, where well-done steaks covered in ketchup dominated the table, I learned that his real name was actually Scott. On top of everything, so to speak, our baseball team had two pitchers and no catcher.

I could no longer ignore the stark writing on the wall. Barely clearing the two-month mark, I suggested we remain friends, and he understood. Was I bummed? Not really. Cuteness can't take priority over compatibility when it comes to dating. And having rejected Christianity, I didn't want to share a bed with one of its confused practitioners. Furthermore, I figured I was still in the dues-paying period of my homosexual evolution. And I continued to pay them.

Despite the romantic frustration, my Las Vegas experience had become one of proactivity, engagement, discovery, and fulfillment — elements noticeably absent two years earlier at my Los Angeles university.

Nowhere did I thrive more than in my work, where I built up my CV in short order. I became arts and entertainment editor within my first year. I attended my first South By Southwest conference in Austin, Texas, which is as close to a pinning ceremony as a young music journalist gets. I became the Vegas correspondent for *Billboard*, and scored other key freelance gigs. I was still just another mid-market alt-weekly critic overly enthused about The Strokes and Moby, but those accomplishments gave me assurance that I had made the right career choice. And I was only too happy to go to work each morning. When I got flustered and forgot those things — or beat myself up for shortcomings, as was my wont — there was an old friend to remind me that while everyone else was just punching the clock or accruing more student debt, I had the dream job.

And that job led to so many other things that gave me strength and satisfaction. It helped me attain new friends and expand my acquaintance network so that even if I went to an event alone, I still usually knew someone there. It allowed me to tick off so many concerts (The Cure! Madonna! Brooooooce!) on my bucket list. And it paid me well enough to grant me one thing that had long eluded my adulthood — a balanced checkbook.

And then there was everything else: the cinephilia I cultivated (even in a movie wasteland like Las Vegas); my markedly improved health; and the openness I developed with my friends regarding my sexuality, one that I nurtured with increasing confidence.

I had, by anyone's measure, turned my life completely around, and then allowed my unique surroundings to shape it into something even better.

And yet, it wasn't enough. Las Vegas wasn't enough.

Homesick, gaysick, and culturesick — and enabled by the ill-reasoned premise that I was fortified enough to flourish in dog-eat-dog Los Angeles — I left my dream job and moved back home, with no concrete plan other than to shake the blues, enjoy my hometown as I hadn't before, and find my boyfriend. For the next three and a half years, I succeeded with the first two directives. Desperation hindered the third.

If Las Vegas was two steps forward and one step back, Los Angeles was walking in place. I was happy but languishing, especially on the job front. Revitalization in one city had given way to paralysis in another. I had destroyed my momentum. I needed purpose. And I desired the warm embrace of a city again.

Just as debt mounted and the relationship I had long clamored for dissolved unceremoniously, the alt-weekly back in Vegas rang. It was a two-fold invitation: Help us cover our new music festival, and consider taking your old job back.

Rewrite

I packed that old duffel bag already knowing the answer. I was gonna give Las Vegas a second chance. It was only fair I repay the favor. ◆

In the Weeds

By Veronica Klash
(Fiction)

Dear Esteemed Members of *Mariposa of Summerlin* Home Owners Association,

Thank you for the notice alerting us to the unsightly and dangerous presence of weeds in our front yard. As you are well aware, we have been a part of this exclusive and illustrious community for many years. In fact, this was the first home we purchased outside of Santa Cruz. I remember walking through the model home, heels echoing in the empty entryway, thinking of all the wonderful upgrades we could include in our new residence. The imported honey-amber marble, the extra-filigree chestnut banisters, the built-in surround-sound home entertainment system. John likes to watch Stanley

Kubrick films the way the great director intended. He calls this "one of life's simple pleasures."

We were grateful to have found a home nestled near others who share our vision and values for how a neighborhood should be. I've often expressed to John the warm sense of belonging that such an exclusive community elicits for me. I only share this so that you, the leaders responsible for upholding that vision and those values, can understand the utmost respect and reverence that we have for the good work you do. And that what you're about to read is in no way an excuse, but simply an explanation.

As I'm sure you know — you've probably seen the billboards and personalized mailers — John is in the midst of launching an exciting new business venture which we are positive will change the landscape of Las Vegas as we know it. Of course, you are all invited to the grand opening gala to be hosted at Red Rock Country Club. This will be a tasteful affair, nothing too lavish. It will be fully catered, with caviar and raw bar, monogrammed swag bags, and a delightful dessert selection provided by Bouchon Bakery, Sprinkles, and Donut Bar. Naturally, I'll introduce you to the mayor, she should know of all the effort you've invested in keeping our city beautiful. She might even help with getting that troublesome nature preserve to allow closer construction for your newest project.

I hired someone to plan this important event, however, I was forced to let her go and take things over myself when she proved to be utterly incompetent. The extent of her inadequacy should've been obvious when she suggested silver-plated flatware instead of gold, but I chose to look the other way, to my own detriment. Finally, I had to step in when she was about to order succulents for the centerpieces. We all know we live in a desert, there's no need for the floral arrangements to reflect or remind anyone of that.

In any case, helming such a momentous evening has been physically and emotionally draining. Tracking the RSVPs alone has been a Sisyphean task. Every time the list seems complete John remembers someone else who was promised an invite. Several times I've woken up in the middle of the night, my head pounding and heart pumping, following a nightmare where the macarons for the swag bags, imported from Parisian bakery Pierre Hermé, don't arrive in time.

Challenges such as those have led to the yard's slipping below our impeccable standards. You see, John normally handles the yard. It keeps him in top physical shape while also maintaining what he calls "the essential bond to our humble and primitive origins." I don't know what he means by any of this, but it seems to make him happy.

However, he's been putting in additional hours preparing this new endeavor. He arrives late at night and I head out early in the morning (there are many details to tackle for the launch, I still haven't finalized our signature cocktail offerings) so I have not had the opportunity to remind him to take care of the horrible weeds in the yard. I've observed their growth closely, slow dotting at first, small green wisps like the first soft tufts on a baby's head. I think the sudden and substantial amount of recent rain has contributed to the full leafy outburst we now have in the yard, particularly in the east corner. My plan is to send John's business partner detailed email reminders regarding the state of the yard. She sees more of him these days. I'm sure she'll encourage him to leave the office and do the right thing.

Thank you for your patience in this matter and for bringing it to my attention.

Sincerely,

Lena Ellson-Smythe

P.S.

You may want to begin an investigation into the color of number 473's stairs. I believe that shade of beige is not approved in the association standards. It appears she has chosen Behr's Premium Plus Ultra in Creamy Mushroom instead of Translucent Silk.

Hello, *Mariposa of Summerlin* Home Owners Association,

It was a pleasure seeing you at the opening gala. I could tell you enjoyed everything that special evening had to offer. It was heartening to see you speak with the mayor for as long as you did. I'm sure that conversation will yield fruits to benefit us all as a community. If nothing else, you were at least able to sample and savor the varied selection provided at the dessert station. The custom created strawberry French toast donuts were a great hit.

This letter is to address the new notice sent about the continued growth invading my front yard. Perhaps you've heard, but John is no longer residing at the house.

Everything has now fallen to me. I'm doing the best I can to adjust to this new situation but will need some understanding and compassion from the association as I navigate this new terrain. He's moved in with his business partner and only stops by to visit the dog. I plan on keeping the dog. I'm aware of the toddler-sized weeds now encroaching in both the east and west sides of the yard. As my father used to say, "we only have ourselves to blame." In earnest, I believed friends would assist me in this transitional period. After all, I have attended many benefits for the causes they champion. But not one of them has offered to come around and pull the weeds. It's up to me and I'm up to the task. I even purchased some Kate Spade gardening equipment to aid in this endeavor, the gloves are particularly appealing with an understated polka-dot pattern in soft mauve.

Enclosed you will find images and documentation refuting the claim stated in your letter that the rare Norwegian Elm gracing my front yard has died. This uncommon breed is deciduous and requires additional time to recover from the frosty winter months. I realize the pale, bare limbs of this proud tree can be deceiving; however, these branches won't remain barren for long. Once you review the attached, I'm sure you'll draw the same conclusion. Your patience is appreciated.

Lena Ellson

P.S.

It seems that you didn't deal with number 473's stairs as the color remains the same. I insist that this issue is addressed. We must maintain consistency in all matters.

To *Mariposa of Summerlin* HOA:

Yes, there are weeds in the yard and the tree still doesn't have any leaves. But right now I'm dealing with much more important issues than the type of plant that is or isn't currently sprouting from the ground on MY property.

I bet you knew this already, but she's pregnant. That husband-stealing, hair-bleaching, silicone-inflated hot air balloon is pregnant. I could turn that scribble he calls a signature into a fresh ink smudge on the divorce papers and she's pregnant.

He doesn't even like kids. He told me he didn't want kids. Who does that to a person? They're naming the bastard John Junior. She'll probably swell to three times her size, and we'll see if he sticks around then. I almost feel bad for her. Almost.

Also, the Kate Spade gardening gloves shredded within the first ten minutes of use and I'm still waiting for the replacements to show up. So I would seriously appreciate some leeway here.

Lena E.

P.S.

I do not appreciate being ambushed by number 473 while unloading groceries in my driveway. I thought that any reporting of transgressions was anonymous and confidential. Where is your sense of discretion? My Three Layer Low-Batch Artisanal Gelato just about melted while she unleashed her rude and uncouth barrage. She would've gotten a piece of my mind if I didn't need to run inside to immediately put the gelato in the freezer.

♦ ♦ ♦

Mariposa of Summerlin HOA

Apparently, we have different definitions of the word 'leeway.' Leeway means cutting someone some slack, not giving them "until the end of the week to sort things out," to quote from your ridiculous letter. You have no idea of what I'm up against.

She showed up at my house last week. That classless common crupina had the audacity to ask me for forgiveness while flaunting her baby bump. Her tears had no effect on me. Maybe that's not entirely true, she did elicit a spasm in my arm which led to the door slamming in her face. I could ensure that kid has no chance of securing a spot in a decent primary school, but I won't.

Instead, I'm tearing out the lawn, the weeds, the tree, everything. It doesn't matter anymore whether the Norwegian Elm can bloom again, I don't want it to. Pancake prickly pear will look just as good. I'm not asking, I'm telling.

Lena

P.S.

I can't be held responsible for my actions if 473 won't stop taking pictures of my lawn.

listen motherfuckers I've had it with the nitpicky bull-shit you can threaten me all you want but know this I was a lawyer before I was a housewife and I will ruin you not in the metaphorical sense but in the very real financial sense so tread very lightly with me you fucking assholes because I can end you in more ways than you can imagine it would be one of my life's simple pleasures now go fuck yourselves I'm planting a fucking cactus

-L

P.S.

that bitch at number 473 can go fuck herself too ♦

Duplex: 5.5.19

By Vogue Robinson
(Poem)

My grandmother is dead
I am no one's baby

I am no one's baby
There is no pillow to land on

No pillow to land on, when the bough breaks
who was the cradle mounted on rockers?

I am without a cradle
a ship over-constructed

Girl, why weep over construction?
Where will I get rest? How will I be repaired?

Duplex 5.5.19

Woman, do not sink in the cost of unnecessary repairs
Do breathe, cool the coals in your throat

Saying it aloud stokes the coals in your throat,
My gramma is dead. ◆

Treading Sand

By Lonn M. Friend
(Nonfiction)

Part One: The Devil, You Say?

"In every city under the sun my name was the axis of the edu-cational circle of religion, arts, and philosophy. Had it not been for me, no temples would have been built; no towers or palaces would have been erected. I am the courage that creates resolution in man ... I am the source that provokes originality of thought ... I am the hand that moves man's hands. I am Satan everlasting. I am the enraged and mute tempest who agitates the minds of man and the hearts of women. And in fear of me, they will travel to places of worship to condemn me, or to places of vice to make me happy by surrendering to my will. The monk who prays in silence of the night to keep me away from his bed is like the prostitute who

invites me to her chamber. I am Satan everlasting and eternal. I am the builder of convents and monasteries upon the foundation of fear. I build wine shops and wicked houses upon the foundation of lust and self-gratification. If I cease to exist, fear and enjoyment will be abolished from the world and through their disappearance, desires and hopes will cease to exist in the human heart. Life will become empty and cold, like a harp with broken strings. I am Satan everlasting."

— Kahlil Gibran

It's November 2001, two months after the towers crumble live on global TV, and the world commences its collective, methodical descent. I'm living in my hometown La La Land emerald westside community of Cheviot Hills with my wife, Joyce, and eleven-year-old daughter, Megan, around the corner from my childhood literary hero, Ray Bradbury, in a million-dollar house I can no longer afford. With a twenty-year music-writing career in professional freefall, priorities are shifting. I'm spiritually evolving, financially dissolving, and constantly wandering — more often than not five hours northeast, up the I-10 and 15 to Las Vegas.

The Ghost Bar sits atop the brand-new Palms Hotel in Las Vegas, fifty-five floors above Sin City's gold-paved streets. Tonight is the pre-opening celebration of this billion-dollar dream of granite, glass, sequins, and shame. The room is wallpapered with jacked-up jesters and dressed-to-the-nines nymphets who tease their slick-rapping wannabe suitors with skintight shakes and halter-top wiggles. I lean against the balcony railing and inhale the crisp night air, basking in the aura of elevation. My stay is brief. This is not my scene, nor my tribe.

Mike, a Jersey-born Irishman who resembles Pussy from The Sopranos, breaks off from his group and heads with me into the night, inspired by his love of Iron Maiden and the promise of a tale or two from the veteran rock scribe. Our destination is Jane's Addiction at the Joint inside the Hard Rock Hotel, where the devil's most perfect playground is playing host to the animated Hebrew whose verse and vice made him a hedonistic hero in the city of angels. Satanic synergy? Stop.

Perry Farrell hops and spins, spitting joy and spirit in an effortless display of choreographed abandon. "You're great!" he affirms to the children, lost and found, who hang onto his words while gyrating to tribal rhythms. Navarro, Perkins, and Martine — the sound machine is soaring this evening. In this time and place where nothing's shocking, I feel my feet leave the floor.

Morning after: Smash cut to same town, different reality. I'm going back home. Red Rock Canyon ribbons the western mountain range, a mere angel's breath away from the Devil's playpen. I travel up Charleston Boulevard until suburbia disappears and nature takes over. I get out of my car. In this primordial bowl sculpted by divinity, the whistle of the wind is the only audible sound. Dinosaurs once walked where I stand; my eyes shut, the faint rumble of ancient thunder works its way into my mind-warp, 120 million years before the first clang of a slot machine. I enjoy a lengthy moment of visual appreciation. Until it's time to roll.

The next offramp on my road less traveled lies dead ahead: Death Valley. Grand, flowing rock of myriad color, shape, and texture, unending testimonials to the Architect. Rod Serling loved this landscape. In *The Twilight Zone* episode "The Lonely," he exiled a convicted murderer to an asteroid to serve out his sentence. This is that asteroid, and I am that exile. Keep moving. Keep breathing. Where I am now is called Dante's View. Six thousand feet above the valley floor, black crows soar at eye level as I sidle up to edge of eternity. On a crystalline day like today, you can see the tip of Mount Whitney in the distance, the highest peak in the lower forty-eight, while in the very next inhale, your gaze is directed down to Badwater, lowest point in God's blessed America. The rise and the fall, harmony of balance, peaks and valleys, truth and lies. Right here, right now. Wow.

It's not enough to merely view the bottom from a crow's nest. Whether you're observing the greed-inspired metropolitan nightmare from a platform of ghosts or an earthen dreamscape from a windswept lookout, you have to go down there. Fears must be faced in both worlds. Let's see just how low I can go.

Badwater is 280 feet below sea level, the geological bottom of this great and powerful nation. The barren, white-salt floor stretches for a hundred miles. The silence deafens. I walk for a while toward the center of the valley — the valley of death — where I stop and plant myself on the hard, smooth basement of time and space. Hello, darkness, my old friend; so, this is where you hang out, huh? Must have had quite a party on September 11. I like what you've done with the place. Very primitive. But you won't mind if I don't hang long.

Numbed by the highway and its hypnotic miles, I arrive home midmorning the next day, weary but empowered. As I pull into my L.A. driveway, I glance at the odometer. Since departing five days ago, I've traveled 988 miles. What does the Tao say? *The thousand-mile journey begins beneath your feet?* Watch that first step. It's a doozy.

Part Two: Exodus

That post-9/11 road trip, replete with its metaphorical significance and freaktown foreshadowing, paved the way for my first desert exile two years later. My marriage ended in the fall of 2003. After twenty years together, Joyce and I had grown apart, our intimate exchanges rare, her patience with me justifiably growing thin. I was one badass breadwinner for two decades, but when my $200,000-a-year job with a record label ended in 1998 and no one called with a new gig, my income plummeted and opportunities for revenue became few and very far between.

I was lost and lonely. At some point, an old friend handed me a book on tape by Dr. Wayne Dyer called *Your Sacred Self*. Early in the New Age narrative, which was all new to me, Dr. Wayne says, "You've been facing the wrong way." I wandered into a yoga studio on the westside and for the next five years sunk into Kundalini yoga, where I learned to breathe fire from the belly, meditate, surrender to the flow of life, and embrace the mystery. Never let anyone tell you that the journey to self is not a selfish sojourn. On October 15, 2003, I hit the road for Southern Nevada, hemorrhaging on the inside, panicking on the outside, praying to the unified field that I'd made the right decision.

So began my first reinvention: treading sand, tapping keys. I landed in a one-bedroom apartment near the corner of Charleston and Town Center, Red Rock Canyon out my kitchen window, Red Rock Resort still three years from groundbreaking. I'd found a land where pilgrims abound, transients and immigrants, lost souls in search of opportunity, fresh starts, reboots, and reinvention. My freelance work brought in a fraction of the funds I commanded back in the affluent days of old. But the pennies on the dollar ignited the holler, and I ventured out into foreign narrative territory, far afield from the rock scribe doing the *Almost Famous* rap on planes, trains, and limousines. Instead, I composed dozens of essays, reviews, and features for a new audience, and in doing so became a more eclectic and evolved writer. I composed most of my first book, *Life on Planet Rock*, during that time.

That first Vegas exile ended on March 24, 2006. Though reorganized, recharged, retooled, and reinvented, I also realized I was just as dazed and confused here as I was in L.A. With my daughter in high school, I returned to L.A. and committed to being a five-star divorced dad. While I still commanded the wages of a part-time Burger King fry cook, life was okay in L.A., and I didn't see myself moving back to Las Vegas.

In August 2012, however, the universe began knocking me for a loop. As I waited for my bus at a well-lit downtown stop, this dude walked up and asked if I had change for a $20. I had on shorts, a white T-shirt, and a KISS Army hat — not exactly the wardrobe of an affluent mark.

"No, sorry," I responded.

Split second later, *BAM!* Something hit me hard on the side of my face. I collapsed and looked up. Now there were four of 'em staring at me. I'm completely flummoxed.

"What the fuck?!" I yelled. *BAM!* Hit again by a fist or a

bat, I have no idea because I never saw the blow. They disappeared around the corner. I was woozy but able to stand. My bus showed up a minute later.

"What happened to you, man?" asked the driver.

"I think I was just mugged," I said. That's when I noticed my wallet and gold necklace (bearing the Hebrew symbol "to life") were gone. Thankfully, I escaped concussion.

Two months later, I got an invitation to spend six months writing at my friend Jimmy's Long Island estate. So I moved my stuff into storage and bought a one-way ticket east. Reinvention, New York-style, right? But the best-laid plans of mice and Friend: Four days after I touched down, Hurricane Sandy scuttled the whole plan. Jimmy's palace was powerless, and the hillsides around his property had turned to drenched marshland. I hunkered down in my pal Neal's midtown flat and rode the storm out.

Meanwhile, back home, my mother was suddenly losing weight, feeling lousy, falling apart at the seams. Two weeks post-Sandy, I was still in Manhattan. Megan, recently graduated from George Washington University with a cum laude diploma, was laboring in uninspired temp jobs in New York. One day she looked at me and said, "Dad, what are we doing here? Let's go home. You can crash on Mom's sofa. I'll find a job in L.A."

Next chapter in the saga? To be the best ex-husband possible. It was nice co-habituating again with my nuclear family. On the other hand, things weren't so good with my mother. I made weekly drives to Oak Park for dinner and *Jeopardy.* Once, she responded to my proclamation, "Look mom, I'm on a journey," with a snappy, "Good for you. Call me when you get there."

With her lifeforce visibly ebbing, I noticed a box of sanitary napkins under the bathroom sink one evening.

"Why?" I asked.

"I've been bleeding," she said. "But I won't go to the doctor. I know what he's going to say! He'll want to put me in the hospital, and if I go into the hospital, I will never come out." A twenty-five-year former Blue Cross employee before she retired in the mid-'90s, Mom loathed the health care industry she knew all too intimately. "They'll take whatever savings I have left. I'm not going to give those bloodsuckers my money. I'd rather die first."

Third week of July 2013, I was packed for a weekend in Las Vegas. My old pal Slash, from Guns N' Roses, was performing with his solo band, three members of whom reside in Henderson. I was loading my backpack in the trunk when my cell rang. "Lonn, I need a blood transfusion," she whispered. "I'm not doing well at all; can you come out and take me to Los Robles emergency room?" I messaged "Happy birthday" to Slash and headed to the valley.

Later, after a blood transfusion, MRI, and biopsy, Mom and I heard the news, oh boy. Cancer. Metastasized and all over the place. The oncologist was an eccentric genius and resident rock star of surgical miracles. His smart phone rang with Aerosmith's — not the Beatles' — "Come Together." I saw this as a promising sign. She was in good hands. Perhaps a miracle was afoot. Two weeks later, however, she entered a seven-hour surgery and passed away on the table after losing her entire body weight in blood twice during the procedure.

"I'm so scared," she had wept as my brother, Rick, and I wheeled her down the hallway to surgery. "Don't be afraid, Mom," I said softly, grasping her hand. "You're going to the Shire." She loved *The Lord of the Rings*, watched the trilogy every time it appeared on cable. Fear never strayed too far from her; fear of dying simply followed fear of living. It's taken years of therapy for me to truly appreciate how long a shadow she cast into my own heart and soul. And how that shadow provides a constant reminder of my own inner light. Mom never remarried and grasped firmly onto remnants of anger from my dad's exodus fifty years prior. In another reality, she'd be dwelling in an oval house cobbled by Hobbits, far away from the 400-square-foot stucco cell she'd spent the last twenty-four years in. But on August 10, 2013, exactly one year and a few hours from my near-death bus stop experience, the Nazgul carried Mom away.

Eleven days after Mom passed, her elder sister, my angel aunt Esther, departed on a different operating-room table on the opposite coast, succumbing to heart failure in Florida.

The day before what would have been my mom's 78th birthday, I attended Esther's funeral at Forest Lawn Mortuary, cradling Mom's ashes in my arms as the rabbi bid the eldest born daughter of William and Annie Shainbaum fond farewell.

I spent the remainder of the month in Mom's pad, going through old letters, books, and files, clues to what made her tick and ticked off. Found a button in her top desk drawer that read, "I'm Much Happier Since I Gave Up Hope." I sorted out the bills and outstanding financial trivialities, shuttling loads of stuff in her 2002 Camry (which I inherited and still drive) to the Goodwill. When I drove into her long-time mechanic's garage and informed him of Mom's passing, the tattooed tough guy raised a black greased finger to his eye and wiped a tear away. The yogis proclaim, "We are nothing but the memory we leave behind." Mom didn't experience an abundance of joy on her journey, but she touched a few folks along the way. Since her death, thanks to vigilant therapy and a lot of writing, I've come to understand and embrace the damage and divinity of my DNA.

In December of 2013, Joyce gently suggested that I find a different place to live. L.A. was too expensive for my hit-and-miss freelance lifestyle. "Why don't you move back to Vegas?" she suggested. "Your dad and brother would love that. It's cheaper, right?" I took her cue and made a drive the following weekend to check out some properties. First place

I looked at, in Centennial Hills, five minutes from Rick's house, they made me an offer I couldn't refuse. My unit was on the far north end of the complex, facing Snow Mountain, with a great view of monsoon lightning storms from the balcony. Hello, Vegas, my old friend. I've come to tread with you again …

Part Three: Palms, Psalms, and the Enduring Qualms

Present day, year six of my second exile. Alanis Morrissette is prancing across the stage of the newly remodeled Pearl Theater at the Palms. She's seven months pregnant, mobile, and radiant. "It's like rain on your wedding day, it's a free ride when you've already paid." My brother is prancing the floor of the casino, recently reassigned from his last successful managerial stint at Red Rock Resort. We tour the Palms' multimillion-dollar facelift, the X static pool, and tower of ghosts, now rebranded as Apex.

Synchronicity struck when Alanis introduced her band, and I recognized the bass player, Cedric Lemoyne. Back in 1999, I accompanied him and lead singer Cinjun Tate, from the band Remy Zero, along with the then-Mrs. Tate, actress Alyssa Milano, to Stonehenge for the day. On the doorstep of the Millennium, we held court with the ancient rock. I sat on the grass, performed Kundalini kriyas, meditated, and wept as the rain fell on my cracking crown. Alyssa took a polaroid of me in the wake of my silent session. There was a visible "glow" in the image about my shoulders. "Look, Lonn, you can see your aura."

I spent time with my dad, seeing movies and listening to him reminisce. I began hitting the voice memo key and recording my piano-playing pop's thoughts and anecdotes about everything from my Polish grandparents to his band opening for Billie Holliday in Sacramento during the '60s.

For the first twenty years of my life, I went to school. For the next twenty years, I went to work. For the last twenty years I went … away. Away from people, purpose, pride, and prosperity. Away from structure, focus, ambition, offices, happy hours, confidence, carnal encounters, and creative consistency. Away from desire, temptation, impatience, irrelevance, idiots, idols, inane conversations, and inauthentic motivations. Moving gingerly through my sixty-third year, I am conscious, clueless, and uncorked to celebrate the next curve.

I haven't cracked $20k since G Dub was president, a man I once reviled but who is, quite frankly, Lincoln and Kennedy combined compared with the night king currently occupying the red, white, and blue throne. I do my damnedest to turn off the news and turn on the muse, letting go of what I can't control, remaining present, grateful for my inhales and exhales. I've also shifted from Kundalini to Yin practice, finding solace and strength in the long, cool poses, ofttimes the lone male in the room at Evolution Yoga. Every morning, I rise to the guided meditations of Vancouver-based poet-healer Sarah Blondin, the only woman whose voice I've heard in my bed at dawn in almost a decade. Her hypnotizing cadence and exquisite psalms for the soul help me kickstart and endure another unscripted day in Paradise. Here's what she said in my earbuds this morning: "You are rising, growing more malleable and stronger, wilder, and more beautiful."

Recently, at the T-Mobile Arena, I watched Florence and the Machine bring the audience to their dancing feet with their cathartic hit single "Shake it Out," a melodic middle finger to the demon who means so much to maintaining the myth of Las Vegas: "It's hard to dance with a devil on your back, so shake him off!"

If I had some grand comeback or redemption story, I'd tell you. I've mastered all the top self-help catchphrases. "The lessons learned are more valuable than the successes or the failures." Or Roethke's timeless adage, "In a dark time, the eye begins to see."

Or, as regards revelation and reinvention and how that's working for me further on down the road, you can't go wrong with this: "The further one travels, the less one knows." Lao Tzu said that 3,000 years ago. What did he know? As it turns out, everything. ◆

The Taste Between Us: A Love Story

By Oksana Marafioti
(Fiction)

The moment I heard the blender, I wanted to destroy my wife. A Pavlov's Dog kinda reaction I had to stifle once again. Instead, I scanned the room for a good place to hide the pizza box. Not because she scared me, but because what she had become did.

I shoved my guilty pleasure under the couch. The space there resisted, already littered with boxes I'd forgotten to throw away, but I pushed and punched and won. For a split second, I felt like a damn champion.

The blender ripped into the vegetables once more.

Feeling gone.

Anxiety.

Alert for footsteps.

For the past year, her obsession with a raw food diet had

haunted our house with its sinister presence, terrorizing any remains of love out of our lives. Or maybe it wasn't the diet. Maybe we've just grown too fond of the taste of resentment.

Every morning was on repeat. After she made her smoothie, she'd come to investigate. Appear in my office, fifteen years of regret trailing on the carpet behind her. In the doorway, she'd tease a sip from the plastic green straw. The matching green mush would disappear between her lips like a parasite about to lay eggs.

Then she'd glare at me, halfway between disappointment and conceit. She'd say, "Tim, I can smell the mozzarella."

My wife had a dangerous sense of smell when it came to cheese.

Like a hyena on the prowl.

But the biggest difference between the animal and Kelly was that she no longer ate the scraps.

"Tim."

From across the room, the icy fingers of her smugness grazed my skin.

I shivered.

It was everywhere. In her tinted blond hair, the painted-on eyebrows and the Botox she'd bought two months back. In her PINK workout leggings and the matching top. She reeked of it. Even her post workout sweat glistened with insidious scorn.

I sat up on the couch. My makeshift bed since she'd

kicked me out of our bedroom. Just as well. Safer. Better for my sense of dignity. The last time I nudged her awake, she dug an elbow into my side with a, "No fucking way I'm having whale sex with you tonight," before rolling over.

"Back from the gym already?" I said.

She cocked her head. "It's almost noon. Don't you have work?"

"Off today."

Her neck looked thin from my vantage point. Skeletal.

"Goody," she said. "And let me guess what you've been up to."

"I'm warning you, Kelly," I said. "Back off." Rage swelled inside my chest. It gave a familiar knock and I opened the door. Welcomed it. This was an old fight, but better be in it than feel like gravel under the tires of a dirt bike.

"Eating that crap again?" she said. "The stink is coming from your pores, Tim!"

I shot to my feet, and she retreated but didn't leave. With one swoop, I grabbed the pizza box from under the couch and threw open the lid.

A challenge.

She shuddered, fingers turning white around her smoothie cup.

"Why do you insist on destroying yourself like this?" she whined. Her eyes trailed my hand as I reached inside the box.

When we first started arguing over our dietary differences,

I thought she was trying to change my eating habits because she cared about my health. That she couldn't stand to see my body expand like a human-sized balloon, gaining weight faster than the scale could handle. I believed she mourned the loss of our restaurant the way I did. That we shared that pain, a catalyst for the way our bodies changed over time. Mine growing, hers thinning.

But lately, that spark in her eyes whenever she threw a tantrum over my comfort eating. Well, it was unnatural. An ominous energy undulated between us now. An energy that I suspected had less to do with my health and more with her denial of what she used to love as much as I did.

I picked up a half-eaten pepperoni slice.

The chords on her neck stood. Neck so elongated it seemed unnatural. Below it, her collarbones were clearly visible. Over the lowcut of her tank, her upper ribs pressed against the film of tanned skin that now more resembled wax paper.

I took a massive bite and she balked.

"So cheesy," I moaned through a mouthful of goodness and offered her the slice.

Goading her this way felt like a triumph. As if an intangible part of me drew great pleasure from the knowledge that an intangible part of her wasn't as immune to the cheese as she let on. One can never bypass one's true nature. Not even with the best of efforts. And the yearning in her eyes betrayed her even as she tried to stifle it.

"You're trying to sabotage my diet; it won't work." She dragged a measured breath. No doubt cleansing. The kind her trainer Chad taught her in all those LVAC yoga classes she'd been digging lately. "Put that away. I can't stand it. I just can't."

"Remember?" I shook the slice in front of her nose. The gesture was tiring on my arm. A thought I shoved away as I concentrated on breaking my wife's will with pizza. "Remember when you could eat an entire large in the span of GOT? The juices running down your chin, riding that pepperoni high like a dragon princess."

"You're a fat asshole." Her voice broke.

Eyes in lockdown with mine, she took a forceful sip of her smoothie, like an assassin shoving a knife into her victim's spleen.

Once, twice …

In response, I devoured my slice. Reached for the last piece. "Look who's pointing fingers. A human can't live on slosh, Kelly, you need help —"

She flung the cup at my head. I ducked. Not fast enough. It hit my shoulder, the lid flying open and spilling kale diarrhea all over my polo shirt.

We used to be happy.

When we first met, the world was a tennis ball. A tennis scholarship got me through four years at UC Berkeley, after all. Kelly was a communication major with her sights set on a career at the *New York Times*. It's like we both knew who we were, the lines of our identities drawn in permanent marker.

Instead of our original dreams, we followed slightly altered versions, but great ones nonetheless. We moved to Las Vegas for Kelly's job, writing an advice column for *Vegas-Posh* magazine. A year later, my restaurant, Prophet, opened to great reviews from Las Vegas' top food critics. By all standards, we were successful.

So how did we get here?

Me a 320-pound, middle-aged ex-business owner turned Uber driver; her an anorexic nurse obsessed with spirulina.

Three words.

Infidelity. Recession. Bankruptcy.

First, I cheated with Gina, my then business partner. Well, not really, but Kelly was set on thinking the worst and I let her. Then Gina stole the Prophet. And finally, bankruptcy — the killing shot.

I remember sitting at the lawyers. Kelly's pen hissed her signature against the surface of the paper like an insect you're too scared to squash. Sweat pooled in the seat of my pants, and I kept thinking, this isn't just us losing our house, cars, everything. This is us, losing us.

Fifteen years out of college and we'd been replaced with unrecognizable versions of ourselves, stuck in a life we crashed by accident.

"Because of you," Kelly liked to point out during those

early days after we'd moved into our rental, "I lost everything."

Guilty as charged.

But a man could change.

I.

Could change.

Or so I thought.

What started off as an attempt to save a crumbling marriage quickly turned into a battlefield. I lost track of who was winning. Not sure I cared anymore. All I wanted was to feel peace.

No, that's not entirely true.

Deep down, I wanted her to stop changing, to see me again as the man she used to respect.

To eat a fucking pizza occasionally.

"I hate you," she said to the slice still hanging from my hand. Her eyes filled with tears.

"Kelly, I —"

She marched out of the office. I heard her slam the downstairs bathroom door and puke into the toilet.

I hovered at the door, stress-eating all the way to the last bite. She never let me in, but still I hovered. The sounds of her retching have become so familiar they seemed normal, just another thing she did on the daily. Brew a pot of coffee. Check out Instagram. Stick a finger in throat. Vomit.

But there was a part of me that refused to accept my helplessness. The desperateness of our situation.

"Kelly, you okay?" I pressed my forehead against the piece of wood that separated us.

She puked again.

And again. Tormenting sounds of an animal in distress.

How was that possible? These days, she was eating more baby food than anything else, for god's sake. Where was that stuff coming from?

"Kelly," I said. "I'm sorry for teasing you. I didn't mean it. I know how important this diet thing is to you ... Can we talk, like really talk for once, without trying to rip each other's heads off?"

Puke, groan, groan, water turning on. Splashing. Water off.

That she wasn't saying anything back was encouraging news. I was a little rusty at relationship-speak, but from what I recalled silence was better than cussing, better than objects catapulting across rooms. It usually meant she was maybe possibly listening.

Maybe.

I went on with a sliver of optimism. "I just want to be happy again, okay? If you want to go back to therapy, I'm in. Seriously. Or we can go to Hawaii for a week. Kinda reset. I'll take some money out of the 401K. Or we can do both. Whatever it takes."

Silence.

"Kelly?"

The door opened a crack. Through it, a green eye stared at me, pupil huge.

"You've never really apologized for sleeping with Gina," I heard her say.

Fuck, I thought. The word kicked my ass every time. I'd shoved my guilt into it, and there was a ton. More than such an inadequate word could contain. I thought and uttered it on the regular, ever since Kelly walked in on me and Gina. For many reasons the stupidest thing I'd ever done, leaving the restaurant door unlocked that night.

"I am sorry."

Did I mean it?

"You don't mean it," she said.

Of course not. I'd apologized many times. For getting caught? For hiding Gina from Kelly? I'm not sure. But words never seemed enough, because "I'm sorry" wasn't what she wanted to hear.

"Tell me what you want."

Resentment filled her eye with tears. "Why can't you admit you fucked her?"

"I didn't." It was true. We never slept together, though we shared experiences that made sex look like a traffic jam. But Kelly would never understand, would she?

I tried to explain a million times, but Kelly needed the lie, so I delivered. "Fine. I should've never slept with Gina. It was stupid and thoughtless and I'm sorry for hurting you like that." But the only thing I regretted was losing the restaurant to Gina afterward.

The one green eye was joined by its twin as the door opened wider.

She smoothly exited the bathroom, as if she didn't just upchuck her entire stomach and a half.

"You want to be happy again?" she said.

"Yes." And this was genuine. But then I quickly added. "I want you to be happy."

We stood face to face. She observed me for a while.

I tried to muster as much genuineness as my eyes could express on such short notice. We either learn from our mistakes or we pretend, right?

Her gaze traveled down my body. Not in a lustful way. More like an appraisal.

She pushed me aside, stumbled down the hall toward the kitchen.

The silence was beginning to make me nervous.

"Where are you going?" I called after her.

"I'm hungry."

Okay, maybe after she eats a jar of peaches & spinach, she'll come to, I told myself as I watched her disappear around the corner.

While anticipating the talk of talks, I found myself sprawled on the living room couch. A luxury these doghouse days. A game of hockey, Golden Knights vs. Jets, was in full swing. The Knights were winning 2-1.

I guess I lost myself in the excitement of the action.

When an arm snaked around my neck, I mistook it for a caress. Until a hand pressed a cloth over my face.

I grabbed her. We struggled. Skinny people can be strong, like bars on windows. I was gaining momentum, but then.

The sweet sterile smell filled my nostrils.

Shapes on the TV grew fuzzy.

The Knights scored the game-winning goal.

A glow radiated from the three iron-wrought pendant lights I'd installed over the restaurant kitchen prep area the previous week. Gina had said it was too extravagant, a needless expense, but I felt the French streetlights vibe got the staff in the right mood to create all those delicious French dishes that gave our place five-star ratings.

Gina called me sentimental. Said I needed to get back to my American roots.

That's how it all started.

That night, the golden glow fell in soft pools over the table where she set up the deep dish she made by hand. To get me back to those roots, she said. We sat cross-legged on the table, facing each other. The pizza disappeared slice by slice, unhurried. The only way to eat a masterpiece. A Pulled

BBQ Pork and Pineapple with three kinds of cheeses masterpiece, to be exact. Our fingers dripped with olive oil and BBQ sauce. We felt no shyness licking them clean.

"This is unfreakingbelievable," I said. The combo of sweet and tangy flavors was so faultless, it gave me a massive gastronomic orgasm.

She nodded, dripping sauce over her cleavage, face flush with joy. The hottest woman I ever did see.

"Better than sex, right?" she said. "Now you believe me?"

"This *is* sex. I've never felt this way before. I don't even know, Gina. Is this sex or love or both? I can't think straight!"

What can I say? Gina brought out the poet in me.

She winked. "Then don't." The grease on her lips glistened and she licked it off slowly. "Just taste." Took another bite, a string of cheese caught in her teeth like a silky thong.

We moaned in unison until we lost the ability to make sounds.

In college, I took a mindfulness class. Our instructor, Mr. Travis, said his priority was to teach us to appreciate the life-altering miracle of meditation. No matter how hard I tried, though, I couldn't find that peaceful place he claimed was just beyond the I-don't-give-a-shit mantra everyone else seemed to get. I just couldn't let go.

But with Gina, I finally found it. My nirvana. On late nights, when we made food together, when we shared our dishes, feeding one another bitesize morsels of our creations, such euphoria flooded me that only one thought floated to the surface of my mind: The tongue must be the path to heaven.

◆ ◆ ◆

The air smelled metallic. A barely distinguishable clanking eased into my ears and then a voice.

"Tim, I can't wait anymore."

The voice sounded familiar, but my head buzzed and I couldn't place it. All I knew was that it was pleasant, the voice. Filled with desire, ripe with promises of home, something I've been craving for so long.

"Tim." More clanking. "I know you're awake."

Sluggishly, I came to. My skin tingled. I'd been dreaming. Or rather remembering those nights with Gina. The dishes we made and gorged on like caterpillars hoarding food for that ultimate transformation. Our metamorphosis.

My limbs prickled with numbness, and at first I thought I'd fallen asleep in the same position. Finally, I opened my eyes against the heaviness of a migraine and squinted at a blurred shape gliding about.

Slowly, Kelly's features swam into focus. The single overhead lightbulb behind her threw sinister signs at the walls of what looked like our basement.

"Finally," she said. "I've been waiting forever."

Still unable to move, I rotated my head left to right, at

least getting some life into me that way.

"What happened?" I rasped.

She walked over to my worktable, returned with a knife. A knife.

My pulse jumped. My head cleared up real fast, the grogginess vacuumed out. I tried to stand up. No luck. "Why am I tied to the chair? What's going on?"

"I'm getting happy," she said. "Like you wanted me to."

I didn't trust the delighted lilt in her voice. It matched the spark of the blade.

"Kelly, honey, what are you doing? I said I was sorry about Gina. Nothing happened. We just ate together."

She swiveled her head toward me. "I've been hungry. For a whole damn year."

"That's what I've been trying to tell you." Hope flashed inside me. "You've been going about it all wrong, honey. Eating that raw shit. You need real food."

"I've been ravenous. Miserable and ravenous. Do you know what that feels like?"

The plastic ties cut painfully into my wrists and ankles.

"Of course you don't," she said. "Scarfing down pizzas with no regard for how that made me feel."

"Kelly —"

She lunged at me and instinctively I jumped. Or tried. I was sure she was about to plunge the knife into my abdomen.

The look on her face was fireworks-gone-wrong. A disaster.

But she did something unexpected. Pressed her nose into the crook of my neck. And took a drawn-out whiff. She rubbed her face against my skin like an animal reading signs. Like instinct, like Kelly had checked out for a moment, replaced by a formidable creature with large globelike eyes and sharp angles.

She trailed her nose down to my armpit. There, her face pushed into the fabric of my shirt and I heard her inhale, as if I were a coke ribbon. "Oh my god!" She groaned with pleasure.

I winced.

"Honey," I said. "I have some pizza left upstairs and I can run and get more, as much as you want. We can celebrate."

"You? Have some pizza? As if all of it belongs to you, like you're some kind of a pizza kingpin?"

"My bad. We have some left. I'll show you." My voice trailed off.

Rubbing her face on my torso, my wife slid to her knees in front of me.

At any other time, the gesture would've made me hard.

It terrified me.

"I can't believe it," she said.

"What, what can't you believe?" I was so epically confused, so uncomfortable and scared. Slightly turned on, too.

Cold panic seeped into my veins, a lethal ivy drip.

"It must be fresh, you idiot," she shouted, making my pulse race.

"Piping hot pizza. Give me fifteen minutes. Tops."

She half moaned in frustration. "After everything that happened you still can't manage to respect my choices."

"Kelly, I don't understand."

She struck her chest with her tiny emaciated fist. "My raw food diet! I've told you over and over, it's important to me. I can't eat pizza."

"All right, all right. I do totally respect that." I realized I was speaking a mile a minute. My teeth chattered, and I bit down hard.

"But I sooo want to," she said. "And you're going to help me." She laid the knife at her feet and rolled up my pant legs. First one. Then the other. "You said you want me to be happy."

I struggled against the ties, but my arms were going numb and I felt weak and out of breath without having moved too much. What a pathetic slob, I thought.

I felt an overpowering urge to cry.

"I do want you to be happy. Just tell me what you want me to do."

One last plea.

She picked up the knife and gazed up at my face. The

Kelly I'd met all those years ago knelt in front of me. Innocent, eager.

"Be still," she said and stuck the knife into my right calf.

I shrieked. A short, panicked sound I didn't recognize. My body shook with the force of it.

Just for a second, I heard her cut deeper into me. Wet, sloppy sounds that robbed me of my humanness. She carved until she held a slice in her hand. It wasn't a large slice, but agony exploded in my every cell as I writhed against my restraints. My skin burned everywhere. With pain and humiliation.

"Are you insane?!"

"It's the only way for us to start fresh," she said with a beatific smile, drawing the blood-dripping slice closer. Her nostrils flared. "You smell delicious. Freshly grated mozzarella, sliced pepperoni, hmm," she inhaled with delight, "pulled BBQ pork, pineapple, OMG Tim! You're amazing."

She bit into the flesh.

Chewed.

Blood spilled out the sides of her mouth, down her neck.

But I couldn't look away. My mouth dried and screaming began to hurt. My vocal chords cracked. I sounded like a snorting bulldog. Paralyzed, I watched her devour that piece, hunched over next to me on the floor. Lick the blood off her fingers, suck it from under her fingernails.

"Another," she whispered. Sliced off the other calf.

And continued. Left thigh, right. Forearm. On and on …

Soon, I had forgotten how to scream. Calmness embraced me. I trusted it. Kelly needed me and I wondered how I'd never realized that I could be her champion. The one person to set her free. All I needed to do was be there for her, body, mind, and soul.

A red puddle blossomed under us. We sat in it like kids in a witchy circle we'd drawn for a seance. For sure, magic floated here with us, and anticipation. But most of all, ultimate bonding.

We'd never been this close before.

Kelly chewed with abandon. "It's been so long since I've tasted anything this brilliant, Tim," she said. When she looked up, her face was transfixed, angelic, eyes large with wonderment. I recognized that look immediately. Nirvana.

She no longer suffered.

In me, she found release. Transformation.

I could give her that much.

A scent of wet iron filled my nostrils. My head swam with fantasies of us, happily skipping down the beach, taking pictures in front of the Eiffel Tower the way we did during our honeymoon. Her moans of contentment, the sweetest soundtrack. We could be that again, I thought I heard myself whisper, but she didn't react as she sliced me to the bone.

Take me, Kelly. I surrender.

I grew lighter. Like when I was a tennis player in college. Any moment now, I'd jump off that chair and return one mean serve.

"Thank you, Tim," I heard her say.

And it was enough. ♦

Love Letter in the Dry Lakebed

By Elizabeth Quiñones-Zaldaña
(Poem)

This is the rest stop.
This is the new mattress.
It's also the zocalo
paved over the dry lakebed
where musicians open guitar cases.

I set my hat on the ground and play
a song carried to the Sheep Mountains,
the Sunrise, and the Colorado River in the south,
the story of love I buried
in the ground for safekeeping
in the years I misread by not reading.

Love Letter in the Dry Lakebed

It's the place we exchanged vows,
and ten years later
a son looks up and asks,
What does "consecrate" mean?

Now let's not pretend
This is something other than it is.
I am tired of inventing work for myself
and calling it a profession.
That kind of faith has forsaken me.
And my buried talents?
The inherited coins — I dug them up,
startled by an encounter with a child
whose hand curled around my finger
was an apology that rang true.
This song had a beginning, and I
a point of entry.

Like most, I learn to play by ear
while plodding through disbelief —
Never write a love letter in a dry lake bed!
that's the message I received.
It's grinding corn into gravel, nothing tender
set apart from thoughtless dust.
This working without a stone to gather

is why hands weep and shed skin concedes:
You're a fool! Never never never —
It's what I heard from the carpeted bedroom floor,
where downstairs someone in front of a screen
fell asleep again, as if to confirm all doubt.
Every petal stripped of wisdom but
here's a dry stalk to chew on,
an invasive flower,
translated from the Latin:
Told ya so.

I wove these messages into lyrics to resist:
My flesh and my heart may fail ...
But the psalm rose to meet me.

Who hasn't waited on a love letter?
Albeit covert as a barista
is happy to see you.
Can't let on. I took a survey

and thought to myself,
Should I go underground?
since I can't go underwater,
since the water slipped away,
since the vow accuses now
as a mirror turned inward.

Love Letter in the Dry Lakebed

It could have been anywhere,
but this is where I discovered
the shared password for the mystic
idol worship of the disillusioned
moral and immoral,
a secret that passes for peace
when the disguise falls.
Twang twang twang,
and a broken string,
Look —

You do not need to test me
to find out about me.
I'm the desert floor
from aerial view.
And that zigzag scar
rising from the navel is
Sola Experientia,
where it came to die.
But not before I insisted,
We must have missed the exit,
pinched myself, woke from dreaming:
in the dry lakebed.
A familiar place.
First, lit signal flares
but later sent postcards

then bought a magnet,
From Fabulous Dry Lakebed.
Old chords don't shake loose
Until they do.

After seven years of little to
no moderation, seven New Years
emerged and I'm here with you,
only now — catching rain in a hat;
like answers preceded by questions,
the word and its meaning
comes by way of new music:
Set apart for a sacred purpose. ◆

Afterword
"The Live-and-Let-Live City"

By Geoff Schumacher

Everybody is acquainted with reinvention. Childhood is all about shaping who we are. We make decisions about who we like and don't like, what we wear, what we eat, what music we listen to, what catchphrases we use. Young adulthood is about determining what kind of work we want to do, what our weekend passions will be, who we want to spend our free time with, and what childhood beliefs we need to leave behind. A successful transition from childhood to young adulthood typically requires a fair degree of reinvention.

In the not-so-distant past, who we became in young adulthood could serve us well enough for a lifetime. The world moved slower then, and our paths were more predictable. One might land a job in young adulthood and stick with that company for forty years. Retirement meant a gold watch and a pension that could be counted on year in and year out for the rest of a life. That's not how it works for most of us today. We encounter opportunities for reinvention throughout our lives.

I decided on a career in the newspaper business when I was sixteen years old. I had been jotting down some really awful song lyrics, as well as a few woefully underdeveloped short stories that read like Dungeons & Dragons campaigns. Although I recognized that these primitive efforts were not ready for prime time, I had caught the bug. I hoped, at least, that I could find a way to one day make a living as a writer. Journalism was my ticket. I got my start at the *Pahrump News*, a long-defunct weekly paper published by a codger named Fred Cook.

Luckily for me, Mr. Cook needed someone to write about high school sports. He wasn't the kind of guy who got out much. Most of the news in his paper was gleaned from press releases delivered to the office and telephone calls. In fact, in the months that I worked for the *Pahrump News*, I don't recall Mr. Cook ever getting up from his chair. Anyway, he put me to work reporting on the teams at Pahrump Valley High School, where I was a student and, incidentally, a participating athlete. He paid me ten cents per column inch. So, if I wrote a story that filled ten column inches, I was paid one dollar. This didn't bother me at the time. I was just getting started, after all, and I was determined to fill lots and lots of column inches. I wrote a lot — on a manual typewriter — and probably took home five dollars a week.

But Fred Cook, whose paper eventually folded, opened a door for me. Before long, I had moved up to the bigger and more professional *Pahrump Valley Times*. Under the tutelage of reporter Joe McCauley and the paper's founder and publisher, Milt Bozanic, I covered a variety of news, but particularly youth sports. I was paid handsomely — $25 per story.

From these modest beginnings I managed to piece together a twenty-five-year career in newspapers. I fully expected it would be a fifty-year career. I would be working in that industry until death or retirement, whichever came first. But sometimes, as some of the writing in this volume of Las Vegas Writes suggests, our best-laid plans run into unanticipated obstacles.

I'm old enough to remember not only when the Internet did not exist, but, more importantly, when the Internet was widely considered to be a toy, a curiosity. Certainly in the newspaper business in the 1990s, the Internet was not seen as a threat — as the Godzilla it soon became, devouring our advertising revenue and crushing our circulation. But by the time I became a daily newspaper publisher in 2011, the full impact of the Internet was starting to materialize. I had reached the pinnacle of my newspaper career at just the moment the industry's foundations were fracturing.

Even then, I did not envision leaving the business. After all, we would make adjustments, learn how to take advantage of the Internet rather than be eaten by it. It was wishful thinking, and unfortunately I spent much of my three years as a publisher cutting expenses, laying off employees and reducing the amount of news and information delivered to readers. It was time to explore other options. I was luckier in this regard than many of my newspaper colleagues. I was able to parlay the skills I had developed as a journalist into a great job in another industry — museums. It was a midcareer reinvention that I could not have envisioned until it happened.

When I think of reinvention, my mind immediately turns to work, but of course that's only one of many ways in which we grapple with change. Each of the contributors to this tenth volume of Las Vegas Writes explores the concept of reinvention from a different perspective.

In a larger context, Las Vegas history can be seen through the lens of reinvention. Las Vegas was a Mormon settlement, a handful of ranches serving travelers, a railroad town, a party house for Hoover Dam workers, a host for World War II and Cold War defense projects, a mob-run gambling resort, and, these days, a diverse metropolis of 2.2 million people that attracts 45 million visitors a year.

It is often said that Las Vegas is in a constant state of reinvention, and I think this is essentially correct. The Strip, downtown Las Vegas, Summerlin, Henderson — wherever you go in this valley, nobody is satisfied with the status quo. This is equal parts exhilarating and maddening. But what makes Las Vegas special is it's a place where reinvention is embraced. As Mike Prevatt explains in his essay, Las Vegas was the best place for him to become his true self. Steve Sebelius' profile of Oscar Goodman reveals a city willing and eager to allow a mob defense attorney to become a mayor.

Las Vegas should be regarded as a city of second chances not only because people come here to escape problematic lives elsewhere. It's also because the city does not pigeonhole any of us. If we want to change careers, reveal our secret selves, pursue our highest ambitions, Las Vegas is open-minded about it, not judgmental. For every complaint I have about Las Vegas — and I have plenty of them — I always include a footnote about how good this city has been to me and my family. If ol' Fred Cook could see how things turned out, I assume he would take some credit for giving me the opportunity to write for his little newspaper at ten cents a column inch. He would be right to do so. ◆

❧ Contributors ❧

Jennifer Battisti, a Las Vegas native, studies creative writing at Nevada State College. Her work has been anthologized in *Legs of Tumbleweed, Wings of Lace, Where We Live,* an anthology of writing and art in response to the October 1 tragedy and is forthcoming in *The Good Fight.* Her worked has also appeared in *Desert Companion, Minerva Rising, The Citron Review, FLARE, Helen: A Literary Magazine, The Red Rock Review, 300 Days of Summer,* and elsewhere. She is a contributing writer for *Las Vegas Woman* magazine. She is the coordinator and a participating teaching artist for the Alzheimer's Poetry Project in Clark County. In 2018, she was the recipient of the Helen Stewart Poetry Prize, and was voted best local poet or writer by the readers of *Desert Companion.* Her first chapbook, *Echo Bay* was released in 2018 (Tolsun Books).

Originally from the Bronx, **Steve Bornfeld** spent decades working for daily newspapers and magazines in New York, Pennsylvania, Tennessee, and, since 1997, Las Vegas. As an entertainment/feature writer, editor, and columnist, his work has appeared in the *New York Post*, *Boston Herald*, *Hollywood Reporter*, and the Gannett and Hearst newswires, as well as locally in the *Las Vegas Review-Journal*, *Las Vegas Sun*, *Las Vegas Weekly*, *Vegas Seven*, *Las Vegas Life*, *Desert Companion*, and *Showbiz Weekly*. He has been honored with multiple state, regional, and national journalism awards from the Nevada Press Association, Best of the West journalism contest, and the Society for Features Journalism. In 2018, he was hired as managing editor/principal writer for LasVegasNewswire.com, produced by the Las Vegas Convention and Visitors Authority. Bornfeld is also a published poet and author of two one-act plays staged at Las Vegas Little Theatre. As a Bronx boy at heart, his only complaint about Las Vegas is he can't take the subway to work.

Harry R. Fagel is a lifelong resident of Clark County, and served for twenty-five years in the Las Vegas Metropolitan Police Department, retiring at the rank of captain. He has authored two books of poetry published by Zeitgeist Press and has been published in numerous anthologies. He received the Hildebrand grant from the University of Nevada, Reno and has been commissioned for a range of poetry projects, both private and public. His album *Wordmurder*, available from Wood Shampoo Records, featured the late Tommy Marth on saxophone. He is currently writing full time, producing poetry, books, performance art, photography, and more. He loves his wife and kids more than anything.

Dayvid Figler is a lifelong Nevadan. He bounces like a manic racquetball ball between the worlds of law (where he's a capital defense attorney) and prose (where he's a professional essayist and storyteller). A two-time Nevada Arts Council Fellow, 2013 Las Vegas Book Festival Crystal Bookmark honoree, and 2019 Medal of Justice recipient from the Nevada State Bar, he finds quirky solace in the third rail of poetry.

Lonn M. Friend writes about music, culture, and life. His first major recognition came during his stint as editor of the music periodical *RIP Magazine* in the late 1980s and early '90s, where he wrote about most of the major music acts of the day, including Guns N' Roses and Metallica. He told the story of those years in his 2006 memoir *Life on Planet Rock*, following up in 2011 with the rest of the story in *Sweet Demotion: How An Almost Famous Rock Journalist Lost Everything and Found Himself (Almost)*. He has also appeared frequently as a commentator for music shows on VH! And E! Entertainment, and in rock documentaries. He has written locally for *Las Vegas Life*, *Las Vegas Weekly*, *Vegas Seven*, and *Desert Companion*, and nationally for *HITS*, *Relix*, *Metal Edge*, *In the Loop* and others.

Award-winning journalist and Nevada Newspaper Hall of Famer **A.D. Hopkins** is a native of Stuart, Virginia, and graduated from the University of Richmond. He moved to Las Vegas in 1969, and during his forty-six-year career worked for all three of Las Vegas' daily newspapers, largely as an investigative reporter and editor. He was founding editor of *Las Vegas Today*, one of the first magazines about the casino industry. He edited *Nevadan* and *Cerca*, magazines published by the *Las Vegas Review-Journal*. He also edited the *Cerca County Guides* series of books, including *Great Hikes, Road Trips, Mountain Biking,* and *Adventures*. He edited many books for Stephens Press, including *Base Camp Las Vegas*. Hopkins co-authored *The First 100*, a history of Las Vegas, and is an authority on early Nevada gunslingers. *The Boys Who Woke Up Early*, his debut novel, was released in 2019 by Imbrifex Books and reflects realities and people Hopkins met as a reporter in the small towns, police stations, and courthouses of Virginia in the 1960s.

Veronica Klash loves living in Las Vegas and writing in her living room. Her fiction work has been published in online literary magazines such as *Cheap Pop* and *Ellipsis Zine*. She is a fiction reader for the University of Nevada, Las Vegas literary magazine *Witness*. Her nonfiction can be found in *Desert Companion*. When she's not writing, Veronica indulges in her other obsessions: food, martinis, and goofy socks. Find more at veronicaklash.com.

Oksana Marafioti is an award-winning American writer of Armenian-Romani descent. Her memoir *American Gypsy* was published in 2012 by FSG. She has published essays and stories in *Time*, *Slate*, *The Rumpus*, *Pilgrimage*, *storySouth*, and several anthologies, including *Immigrant Voices* (Penguin Books, 2015). She is a 2013 Library of Congress Kluge Fellow and a guest lecturer at the University of Nevada, Las Vegas.

Mike Prevatt is a Los Angeleno by blood but a Las Vegan at heart. After frequent visits as a teenager and college student, he relocated to the Las Vegas Valley in 1998 and began his professional journalism career at alternative weekly *Las Vegas CityLife*, where he began covering local musicians and became the first local journalist to cover the Strip's DJ and nightlife scene. After a brief hop back to Los Angeles, he returned to Las Vegas and *CityLife* at the dawning of Downtown's Fremont East scene, where Mike immersed himself in its musical and lounge/DJ scene. He moved to *Las Vegas Weekly* in 2013, covering a greater range of topics, and then transitioned to radio producer at KNPR in 2019. Mike is still an avid concertgoer, as well as a fussy cinephile and an unabashed roller-coaster enthusiast. You can follow him on Twitter at @mikeprevatt.

Elizabeth Quiñones-Zaldaña earned a B.A. in English from the University of Nevada, Las Vegas. Her poetry has been published in *From Snowcaps to Desert Flats: An Anthology of Latino Writers in Nevada*; *Legs of Tumbleweeds, Wings of Lace: An Anthology of Literature by Nevada Women*; *Clark: Poetry from Clark County, Nevada*; and *300 Days of Sun*. Her chapbook, *Bougainvillea*, is forthcoming in August 2019 from Tolsun Books. She lives in Southern Nevada with her husband and three children.

Vogue Robinson was named Clark County's second-ever poet laureate in 2017, and she currently serves as executive director of the nonprofit Poetry Promise, Inc. Robinson is a graduate of San Diego State University, where she earned her BA in English. Vogue has been working with the valley's Battle Born Slam team since 2013, and has represented Vegas at four national competitions. She is the author of *Vogue 3:16* and her work has also been published in *Clark, Desert Companion, Red Rock Review*, and *Legs of Tumbleweeds, Wings of Lace: An Anthology of Literature by Nevada Women.*

Erin Ryan has seventeen years of clips in her garage, about half wrapped up in Las Vegas. As a writer and editor for newspapers and weekly magazines, she has been recognized by the Society of Professional Journalists, Best of the West, and state press associations in Idaho and Nevada. As a freelancer, she fine-tunes a little of everything and tells stories for outlets ranging from *Travel + Leisure* and Guardian Media Group to *Las Vegas Magazine* and *Desert Companion*. Off the page, she is mom to an ancient dog and a brand-new human.

Steve Sebelius has covered government and politics for nearly thirty years in California and Nevada, writing for daily and weekly newspapers and television stations. He's currently the politics and government editor for the *Las Vegas Review-Journal*, where he writes a weekly column on Nevada politics. He's also the political analyst for 8NewsNow, the Las Vegas CBS affiliate, where he co-hosts the weekly show *PoliticsNOW*. Sebelius graduated from Biola University in La Mirada, California, in 1989. He worked for the *Huntington Beach Independent*, the *Pomona Progress-Bulletin*, the *Sacramento Union*, the *Las Vegas Sun*, the *San Bernardino Sun*, and *Las Vegas CityLife* before being hired to write political columns for the *Las Vegas Review-Journal* in 1999. Sebelius also served as the editor of *CityLife* from 2005-2011.

Amanda Skenandore is the author of two historical novels, *The Undertaker's Assistant* and *Between Earth & Sky*, winner of the 2019 American Library Association's Reading List award for Best Historical Fiction. She lives in Las Vegas with her husband and their pet turtle, Lenore.

Scott Dickensheets is the deputy editor of *Desert Companion*, the magazine of Nevada Public Radio. Before that, he top-edited *Las Vegas CityLife* and the *Las Vegas Weekly*, served as managing editor of *Las Vegas Life*, and worked in a number of positions at the *Las Vegas Sun*. Dickensheets has edited, co-edited, or contributed to eight previous volumes of the Las Vegas Writes series and was an assistant editor of *Nevada: 150 Years in the Silver State*.

Geoff Schumacher is the senior director of content for the Mob Museum in Las Vegas, responsible for its exhibits, artifacts and public programs. He earned his bachelor's degree in journalism from the University of Nevada, Reno, and his master's degree in history from Arizona State University. He had a twenty-five-year career in journalism, with stops at the *Las Vegas Sun*, *Las Vegas CityLife*, *Las Vegas Mercury*, *Las Vegas Review-Journal* and *Ames* (Iowa) *Tribune*. He is the author of *Sun, Sin & Suburbia: A History of Modern Las Vegas* and served as editor of *Nevada: 150 Years in the Silver State*, the official book commemorating the state's sesquicentennial. He is associate editor of the *Nevada Historical Society Quarterly* and has edited, co-edited or contributed to seven editions of the annual Las Vegas Writes anthology for Nevada Humanities.

About Huntington Press

Huntington Press is a specialty publisher of Las Vegas- and gambling-related books and periodicals, including the award-winning consumer newsletter, *Anthony Curtis' Las Vegas Advisor.*

Huntington Press
3665 Procyon Street
Las Vegas, Nevada 89103
LasVegasAdvisor.com
e-mail: books@huntingtonpress.com